The Evolution of Self-Help

The Evolution of Self-Help

Matthew E. Archibald

First published in 2007 by
PALGRAVE MACMILLAN™
175 Fifth Avenue, New York, N.Y. 10010 and
Houndmills, Basingstoke, Hampshire, England RG21 6XS
Companies and representatives throughout the world.

PALGRAVE MACMILLAN is the global academic imprint of the Palgrave Macmillan division of St. Martin's Press, LLC and of Palgrave Macmillan Ltd. Macmillan® is a registered trademark in the United States, United Kingdom and other countries. Palgrave is a registered trademark in the European Union and other countries.

ISBN-13: 978–0–230–60037–9
ISBN-10: 0–230–60037–9

Library of Congress Cataloging-in-Publication Data

Archibald, Matthew.
        The evolution of self-help / by Matthew E. Archibald
            p. cm.
        Includes bibliographical references and index.
        ISBN 0–230–60037–9 (alk. paper)
            1. Self-help techniques—United States—History. I. Title.

BF632.A37 2007
361.4—dc22   2007006258

A catalogue record for this book is available from the British Library.

Design by Newgen Imaging Systems (P) Ltd., Chennai, India.

First edition: December 2007

10 9 8 7 6 5 4 3 2 1

Printed in the United States of America.

To my mother and father

Contents

List of Tables and Figures

Tables

Figures

Preface

This book is about the evolution of self-help movement organizations in the United States. The dramatic rise and ubiquity of self-help during the mid- to late twentieth century positions it high among other healthcare institutions such as drug rehabilitation, the health maintenance organization (HMO), and patient rights as an integral part of the landscape marking our daily lives. Self-help support groups and organizations have emerged as the primary way of alleviating a number of medical, behavioral, and psychological problems and it is largely taken for granted nowadays that sufferers of chronic conditions like Lupus, Parkinson's, or alcoholism will join together to create organizations to overcome the devastation wrought by these illnesses. Self-help in its various forms is embedded in our national culture and a considerable body of excellent research has been devoted to understanding its importance, especially the novel organizational form known as the self-help group—member-designed and -operated psychotherapeutic support groups for people who experience a common illness or condition ranging from alcoholism to cancer.

I began to study self-help in the early 1990s as an ethnographic project in one of Howard Becker's graduate seminars. Attending graduate school by day and support group meetings at night, the three things I quickly learned were, first, I was not much of an ethnographer despite the many hours I spent in the field observing self-help meetings and talking to its practitioners; two, my putative subjects, self-help members themselves, were already self-reflective enough to circumvent my pigeonholing them—they knew what they were up to and why; and three, these group members turned out to be the most courageous and genuine men and women I had ever met. In order to understand what they had accomplished, and to better place what I was seeing and hearing in the context of the broader self-help movement that swept the United States in the 1970s and 1980s, I read through as much of the self-help literature as possible. While group members had riveting stories to tell about their own lives, the history of the group and its members, I still sought answers to some basic questions about the growth of the movement that were not immediately accessible either by way of my informants' experience or through self-help studies conducted during that time. My interlocutors' wry observations that "everybody's in self-help these days," stimulated my curiosity to know more precisely how many people there actually were in self-help, how many groups existed, what missions were served, how long self-help had been around, where it got its resources, and why it was so popular. Books and articles by Thomasina Borkman, Leonard Borman, Mark Chesler, Keith Humphreys, Alfred Katz, Linda Kurtz, Greg Meissen, Thomas Powell, Frank Riessman, and a long list of others answered many of these questions but remained vague with respect to what I continued to think were some basic research issues that needed to be raised about a phenomenon that had arisen so quickly and left such an indelible mark on American culture. Instead of focusing on my initial interests in group processes related to identity reconstruction, cooperation, and status hierarchies, I began to wonder about the larger population of self-help organizations, the movement itself. That there was a gap seemed odd because for all of our knowledge about self-help, the generic "self-help group" and even about specific organizations such as Alcoholics Anonymous and the National Alliance for the Mentally Ill, a key question remained unanswered: How did this population evolve and where did it get its resources to do so? To answer the question required complete information on all the groups and organizations that had existed, and, although White and Madara (2002) had been selflessly putting together something of a master list of self-help sources for a couple of decades, no such information was available. At this juncture, a radical shift in the direction of the project took place.

Using White and Madara as an inspiration and guide, I began the three-year task of creating a dataset that contains information on the life histories (including e.g., founding and dissolution dates, market niche, membership, professional legitimation, political affiliation, services, and so forth) of 589 national self-help organizations active between 1955 and 2000. While these are not all self-help organizations that exist, they are as many as I could locate with documentation relevant to the questions at hand. Consequently, researchers in the health and social sciences can now investigate with considerable accuracy the evolution of national self-help organizations, track public and professional recognition of these collectives, and investigate resource use over time, among other applications. The availability of this novel aspect of this study, the original database of life histories of active national self-help organizations, is like discovering a new archival source: we can ask questions about prominent examples of organizations contained in the dataset such as The Compassionate Friends, Mended Hearts, and Depression After Delivery, we never could before.

I begin this book by chronicling the processes of growth, decline, diversification, and resource partitioning among self-help organizations, and then describe how self-help attains legitimacy and institutional standing. Doing so is not uncontroversial. Most self-help researchers are interested in how groups do the things they do. It is at this level that we are most intrigued since groups and their members are the driving force behind the self-help phenomenon. Yet, as social scientists know, groups are not static phenomena. Invariably, over time, they evolve more or less structured ways of doing the things they do in order to be more effective, to be more efficient, to survive and flourish. Consequently, I have focused on the evolution of self-help, beginning not with the first group of, for example, a meeting of wives of alcoholics or parents of children with Down's Syndrome, but with the first national organizations, the more formally structured expression of the groups. The choice means that this book does not analyze the spontaneous and informal aspects of self-help groups, although that is certainly a crucial part of self-help organizations, but rather the evolution of the movement. I focus on how the movement was able to cultivate legitimation and acquire resources, to recruit not only new fellow sufferers to its groups but new groups as well, and to grow and flourish. To capture this process, I explore the histories of several individual self-help organizations, and then, drawing on the larger database of all organizations, present a picture—usually in the form of graphs—of the entire movement as it changed over time. The point is to describe the demography of self-help—how this novel social institution evolved over a forty-five-year period.

In the end, one should come away from the discussion of self-help understanding first, that although self-help consists of voluntary groups, it evolves just like other kinds of organizations in such a way that, second, it ultimately seeks to be recognized as a legitimate collective enterprise by mainstream authorities and constituents alike, and, therefore requires the same kinds of resources other organizations need in order to develop. And yet, self-help has ways of acquiring legitimacy and using resources that distinguish it from other kinds of collective enterprises. It remains a unique solution to the problem of chronic illness and its history provides grounds for cautious optimism about the direction of healthcare practices in the United States. Where my explanations remain unclear and obscure, I hope that this is due to the complex nature of the thing I am studying and not bad writing, or worse, muddled thinking. Many people have tried their best to help me avoid the latter two pitfalls, and any shortcomings that remain are mine, not theirs.

Acknowledgments

I owe a great deal of thanks to members of all the self-help groups who have talked to me and who, by dedicating themselves to the noble task of facing rather than fleeing their physical and mental conditions, often terminal in nature, have shown great courage and humanity. Although this book analyzes self-help en masse, I have benefited greatly from years spent observing individual self-help support groups in action. The collective good that they achieve for both members and society at large cannot be emphasized enough. I am highly indebted to a number of colleagues and peers, as well as a handful of anonymous reviewers, who have proven incisive critics of my research in various stages including Stanislav Dobrev, Marc Schneiberg, Meyer Zald, Arjen van Witteloostuijn, Tim Dowd, Sarah Soule, Joel Baum, Cathy Johnson, Wendy Simonds, Thomasina Borkman, Glenn Carroll, David Meyer, Patrick Coy, Wolfgang Bielefeld, Holly McGammon, and John McCarthy. I am especially indebted to Debra Minkoff, Gary Hamilton, Pete Guest, Judith Howard, Amy Benson, and Cynthia Hinton who read the earliest, most chaotic, versions of this research and helped fashion it.

As a truly collaborative project, I owe more thanks than I can render to my research assistants Kim, Sasha, Kirsten, Bryn, Kristen, Karen, and Amanda who collated data, hunted down references, dug through archives, read drafts of papers and chapters, and shaped the project with their curiosity and insights. I thank the National Science Foundation for their generous assistance in providing me with a Dissertation Grant (62-5041) at a crucial juncture in the data collection.

I am immensely grateful to Gabriella Georgiades and Joanna Mericle my editors at Palgrave Macmillan, for their commitment and faith in this project. The two of them really did a remarkable job of shepherding the manuscript through various stages of development.

Lastly, my deepest thanks go to loved ones and family, my mother and father, Sarah, Melanie, Eric, Marlene, Suzanne, Lisa, John, Cliff, Ed, Tim, and Anne who cheerfully tolerated my self-absorption all these years.

I
The Demography of Self-Help

The ongoing debate about the decline of civil society conceals a seldom-noticed phenomenon in sociological and political discussion. Arguments that associational life in Western polities has taken a Hobbesian turn, that social institutions such as family, community, neighborhood, and social club are in crisis, and that civic disarray reflects the failure of Western democratic institutions, frequently discount the emergence of new types of voluntary organizations and new organizational sectors (Ladd 1998; Skocpol 1996). Historical evidence suggests that voluntary associations come and go, reflecting societal-level selection processes that result in new configurations of organizations. For instance, during the 1960s and 1970s, decreasing medical-professional hegemony and increasing rationalization within the healthcare system, privatization in human services, the ascendance of group psychotherapy, and the so-called medicalization of society all contributed to the unprecedented expansion of community-based health and human service organizations and movements, many promoting complementary and alternative healthcare (Conrad 1992; Scott et al. 2000; Scheidlinger 2000; Wolch 1996). Drug and rape crisis clinics, legal and medical coops, halfway houses and shelters experienced widespread popularity.[1] Under the auspices of a broad consumer health movement, the civil sector witnessed rapid expansion of a variety of alternative healthcare social movements including New Age counseling, chiropractic and naturopathic medicine, and acupuncture (Goldstein 1992). The most well-known of these was self-help: member-designed psychotherapeutic support groups for people who experience a common illness or condition ranging from alcoholism to cancer.

Seemingly overnight, self-help "evolved from an oddity and suspect human service to a vigorous, diverse endeavor known to all who watch daytime talk shows" (Lieberman and Snowden 1994:32). Throughout the 1980s and 1990s, forums for discussion of self-help emerged in a wide range of media. Mainstream academic and medical journals such as the *Journal of the American Medical Association*, and the *New England Journal of Medicine* devoted serious attention to self-help and popular magazines and the press featured stories about self-help members. Clearinghouse listings of organizations available for self-help grew steadily (White and Madara 2002), while social service agencies regularly referred clients to any number of self-help groups (Kurtz 1997). Significantly, the federal government weighed in by funding research and developing programs designed to evaluate the efficacy of self-help services. In 1987, Surgeon General Everett Koop's Workshop on Self-Help and Public Health, under the auspices of the Department of Health and Human Services, promoted self-help among federal and state and public and private agencies, predicting it would become the "other" health system in the United States (Margrab and Millar 1989).

It should come as no surprise then that membership in self-help support groups in the 1980s and 1990s blossomed dramatically. Estimates of participation vary, but the number of Americans involved in self-help groups remains considerable. For instance, 12.5 percent of Wuthnow's (1994) sample participated in self-help, amounting to between 8 and 10 million people. Nash and Kramer's (1994) estimates range from 6.5 million to 14 million participants. Mullen (1992) puts the number between 10 and 15 million, while Davison, Pennebaker, and Dickerson (2000) cite 1997 epidemiological figures that place lifetime participation at around 25 million. For comparison's sake, the number of American workers who were union members in the 1990s hovered around 16.5 million (*World Almanac* 1996).

Self-help is now largely taken for granted in the United States. Bookstores and libraries contain extensive self-help sections (often larger than scholarly areas such as economics, political science, anthropology, and sociology). Radio, television, film, and the popular press all reference self-help without the aid of additional definitions. The dramatic rise and ubiquity of self-help places it high among other healthcare institutions shaping our daily lives.[2] Self-help support groups have emerged as *the way* of solving a number of medical, behavioral, and psychological problems and it is largely expected nowadays that sufferers of chronic conditions like Lupus, Parkinson's Disease, or alcoholism will fashion organizations to manage if not overcome these devastating illnesses. The image of a mid-sized coterie of men and women meeting in a church basement, public library, or hospital lunchroom confronting the debilitating stigma of their condition, illness, or problem, or that of a relative or loved one has become familiar to all who are attentive to any manner of contemporary media. Yet, media attention tends to be self-reinforcing as it echoes from books to newspapers to talk-shows to films. The analytic difficulty in determining the prevalence of self-help is confounded by the burgeoning of media representation of self-help that poorly reflects the changes in the essential components of it: that is, the organizations and groups that meet throughout the country. One of the crucial barriers to mapping self-help organizational growth is that self-help is too often a vague term referencing ideologies, books, and programs, in such a way as to seem to be all things to all people (Riessman and Carroll 1995). But self-help would remain only a literary genre without the groups, meetings and organizations that constitute it (Borkman 1991; Schubert and Borkman 1991).

Fortunately, several decades' worth of research featured in work by Borkman (1991, 1999), Humphreys and Rappaport (1993), Katz and Bender (1976), Katz (1993), Makela (1996), Powell (1987, 1990, 1994), Rice (1996), Riessman (1985), Riessman and Carroll (1995), and Taylor (1996), among other prominent social scientists, has broadened our understanding of self-help organizations and groups immensely. Self-help research has detailed the central characteristics of its organizations and groups, and even includes a few preliminary epidemiological studies of local organizational populations. However, little is known about the growth, decline, and persistence of the population of national self-help in the United States, or about the social, cultural, and political forces shaping the evolution of this population. Gaps in our knowledge of the dynamics of the organizational population of self-help is curious in light of continuing declines in external resources available to self-help, which has been noted (not without alarm) in the self-help literature (Hedrick, Isenberg, and Martini 1992). In 1989, the Minnesota Self-Help Network closed, and, in the 1990s, New York City and New York State clearinghouses closed. Around this time, Illinois cut back its staff and Massachusetts, Connecticut, and Michigan all suffered funding setbacks. Since self-help organizations are dependent on such resources, decreasing external support might have suggested to researchers the possibility of a more general decline in the self-help population of organizations itself, worthy of investigation.

Knowledge of self-help can be advanced by examination of the fundamental changes in the demography of the movement. Despite extensive understanding about the self-help movement (Katz 1993), the generic "self-help group" or even about a specific organization such as Co-Dependents Anonymous, important questions that remain unanswered range from basic demographics like how many national self-help organizations are there, what conditions do they treat, and how long do they last to sociopolitical mechanisms of institution-building such as who supports them and what kinds of resources do they use?[3]

Given the representation of self-help as "here to stay" (Katz 1993), that is, the fact of its institutional status as *the way* to organize social support, there is a real need for research addressing the organizational evolution of self-help.[4] By emphasizing the organizational components of the self-help movement, the issue of the growth and decline of this cultural phenomenon can be examined as the question of the growth and decline of self-help movement organizations. Consequently, this book focuses on the organizational components of self-help in order to provide the foundation for understanding the societal-level processes shaping the institutionalization—taken-for-grantedness—of this form of organization.

In this book, "self-help" refers to self-help organizations, specifically, national self-help organizations. These organizations address personal stigmatizing conditions ranging from medical disability to behavioral dysfunction, in a public but intimate face-to-face group setting. Stigmatizing conditions and their constituencies might entail alcoholism (Alcoholics Anonymous), amputation (National Amputee Foundation), cancer (Reach to Recovery), or sudden infant death syndrome (National SIDS Foundation). Organizational focal problems cover, but are not limited to, mental illness, drug addiction, gambling, codependency, child and infant mortality, anxiety, phobia, autism, physical handicap, neurological pain, paraplegia, head injury, infections, autoimmune disease, and diabetes. They also involve other stigmatizing conditions such as adoption, divorce, and sexual orientation. The importance of studying self-help organizations is that: "changes in the number and types of provider organizations reflect changes in our beliefs and ideas about what kind of service healthcare is and how it should be provided" (Scott et al. 2000:25–26). That these types of member-controlled organizations arose to address gaps in healthcare services reveals much about the overburdened healthcare services in the United States in the late twentieth century.

A central motivation of this book is to understand how marginalized practices become mainstream. I do so by examining the diffusion of the organizational components of the self-help movement. Organizational analysis helps avoid the tendency to overemphasize the burgeoning of self-help as a question about individuals—why do people, particularly the kinds of people in these groups, believe the things they do and do the things they do—rather than as a question about how social action (self-help groups) becomes a way of life. One way that marginalized practices become mainstream is through changes in ideologies. There is a good deal of research about how self-help ideologies reflect those of the broader culture (e.g., Rudy and Greil 1988). For example, the particularly American notions of self-reliance and self-sufficiency resonate clearly in do-it-yourself healthcare in the form of the self-help group. But what is it about these organizations (and the movement in general) that makes them the vehicle by which an entire way of life emerges? This question remains puzzling since there has been no systematic research on the population of self-help organizations. To address the issue, a comprehensive source of data on self-help organizations had to be developed.

In the late 1990s and early 2000s I created an original database of life histories of all active national self-help organizations in the United States between 1955 and 2000. With this database, we can ask questions about self-help we never could ask before. Two of these questions are basic to any study of the demography of organizations: What are the dynamics of self-help (e.g., how many organizations are there, what conditions do they treat, how long have they been around, who supports them, what kinds of resources do they use, etc.) and what social forces influence these dynamics? The story that unfolds in this book details the emergence, growth, and persistence of self-help.

To provide a brief preview of what follows, a central idea I examine is that self-help resembles other social movement, commercial and noncommercial organizational populations in that there is a strong tendency toward exponential growth followed by marked decline and stabilization over the long run.[5] Most importantly, for self-help this pattern is linked to two fundamental mechanisms by which new organizational forms—organizations with similar features—diffuse across a population and become institutionalized or taken-for-granted: the processes of legitimation and competition. Legitimation (or public recognition) facilitates movement growth by making creation of self-help organizations the norm while competition shapes its longevity by limiting resources to certain ones. A demography such as the one developed in this book provides a wealth of new knowledge and helps make sense of underlying ideological and material forces shaping the evolution of this particular movement.

In the other direction, understanding the diffusion of self-help organizations has implications for complementary and alternative healthcare by uncovering societal-level selection processes that generate new configurations of organizations. The kind of diffusion model used in this study applies to a broad range of organizational populations (Carroll and Hannan 2000), but the way in which the model works through legitimation and competition is determined by the specific kinds of organizations to which it is applied, in this case, health social movement organizations. For example, in commercial populations, diffusion of organizational forms and legitimation follow from connections that organizational entrepreneurs have with mainstream authorities in business and politics. Challenger groups, in contrast, do not automatically have these connections, which is why they are often referred to as "non-institutional actors"; they operate outside mainstream authority. They challenge mainstream healthcare authorities and bring about socio-legal and cultural change in the way we practice health in this country.

The implications for the study of social movements are significant. Among fundamentalist, globalization, environmental and gay rights movements, the health movement may arguably be the most important collective action taking place today. The list of movement foci or sub-movements under the broader rubric of actions aimed at challenging the status quo in healthcare is long (see Brown et al. 2004). It includes but is not limited to: the breast cancer movement, AIDS activism, the women's health movement, stem cell research, the recovery and self-help movement, disability rights, environmental activism aimed at the health effects of environmental degradation, complementary and alternative health movements including new age practices, antismoking and obesity campaigns, movements against genetic modification of food sources, and so on. Understanding the forces that give rise to self-help and that facilitate its institutional standing helps us understand these movements as well. Moreover, many putative non-health movements contain wings that have health orientations, so that knowing about the evolution of self-help sheds light on these other movements.

Self-Help Organizations

Self-help passes through stages on the way to becoming fully orga-nized; beginning with its small informal groups, it experiences increasing complexity as more members create more groups. This leads to a greater division of labor and a more systematic (formal) way of conducting business (Donaldson 1996). Self-help is strongly goal-oriented and consists of programs that are sustained by an increasingly differentiated, complex organizational structure (Powell 1990).[6] Most importantly, the core social "technology"—*the way* in which self-help carries out the work of mutual aid—depends on an organizational structure that sustains the informal groups, meetings, chapters, and affiliated networks by which self-help is known and through which it recruits its members. The social technology of mutual aid is in fact the most salient characteristic of self-help. It consists of a small-group setting where members share stories and information concerning their personal experiences dealing with stigmatizing conditions in order to assist themselves and others in overcoming their problems. This technology of self- and mutual support is a ubiquitous characteristic of the self-help organizational form. Self-help organizations promote a philosophy of mutual-aid, individual self-determination, autonomy, and dignity based on this intimate way of conducting business. The result is a shared understanding of members' focal problems, needs, and concerns. In addition, the ideological principle of individual and group self-determination becomes the underpinning for a movement that opposes the medical hierarchies of the dominant healthcare system.

Throughout the book the appellations "self-help" and "self-help movement" are used to connote national health movement organizations. In this context, the term self-help refers to national self-help organizations because local self-help groups are the components of these larger entities, and, invariably attempt to establish a national presence in order to reach as many potential members as possible who share their condition. As I discuss in more detail in the following chapter, national self-help organizations, in contrast to local unaffiliated groups, promote well-developed support programs among local chapters, meetings and groups, provide stability and predictability, and have a more diverse membership and a stronger leadership structure (Powell 1987, 1990). Also, national self-help organizations are recognizable to a broader audience than strictly local organizations, which translates into a larger constituency. By defining self-help as such, it becomes easier to investigate the evolution of self-help movement organizations, since national organizations have an established presence and can bring about change in healthcare at a societal level.

Self-Help and Health Movement Organizations

Because framing self-help in health social movement terms has its pitfalls (see Chapter Two for a complete elaboration), most researchers and practitioners tend to think of self-help groups and organizations as largely apolitical, which is in part correct. Self-help groups differ importantly from other kinds of voluntary associations, particularly social movement organizations, with regard to their ostensible public role (i.e., goals). The latter seek social, legal, and political change and provide public services while self-help seems to be oriented largely toward personal, rather than societal, transformation. Indeed, self-help organizations do not originate with a justice frame or an orientation toward righting sociopolitical wrongs. Their focus is on providing support, broadly construed for members, first and foremost. In this way, self-help differs from social movements, such as those aimed at globalization, war, or environmental issues. It also differs from health movements such as the disability rights movement that frame their activities in terms of the provision of civil rights, although some organizations, NAMI, for instance, are instrumental in advocating for its members' civil rights. Like these other movements, it challenges authority on multiple levels, uses similar strategies, and implicitly promotes social and cultural change.

Self-help acts as a grassroots movement. It offers social support that may not be available from other sources such as family, friends, neighbors, community, or other social and religious institutions (Katz 1992b). Control of organizations by group members is a defining feature of self-help (Kurtz 1997). It is organized outside of traditional institutional domains (such as medicine), and its ethos of self-care implicitly contradicts medical professional authority ringing changes. Constituents disillusioned with the dominant healthcare system can design their own healthcare service delivery mechanisms in the form of self-help groups (Borkman 1991; Katz 1993; Powell 1994; Riessman and Carroll 1995). The formation of self-help groups to contend with problems ranging from lupus to spina bifida to drug addiction threatens conventional authority structures in these areas. For example, women with post-partum depression have found it necessary to create non-medically-affiliated groups (e.g., Depression After Delivery) with which to cope with the stigma of depressive and sometimes psychotic episodes following childbirth, rather than relying on the medical profession (Taylor 1996). Organizations such as Self-Help for the Hard of Hearing, The National Alliance for the Mentally Ill, Disabled in Action, SHARE-Self-Help for Women with Breast and Ovarian Cancer, and other breast cancer and mastectomy groups, also operate beyond the purview of mainstream healthcare.[7]

Self-help challenges and confronts institutionalized healthcare in that it "draws on the embodied illness experience and the body as a counter-authority to medicine and science" (Zavestoski et al. 2004:269). Like other health movements, it pits experiential knowledge, found in group members' personal stories, against theoretical knowledge generated by institutional authority through disease narratives. These narratives challenge science, politics, business, and other institutional domains that control health knowledge and practice. They also foster the collective and therefore, public, experience of illness. This is a compelling idea: although individuals join self-help organizations in their personal search for rehabilitation, collectively they provide a public service. Hence, the emphasis on self-help/mutual aid (Borkman 1999). This implies that while self-help organizations appear to be expressive organizations—organized to provide a benefit for members (Marx and McAdam 1994)—their consequences, as collectivities, are not infrequently political and have wide-ranging effects on our national culture.

Self-help also reshapes the healthcare sector by defining itself in opposition to mainstream healthcare, and smuggling alternative practices into the field under the auspices of egalitarian beliefs about what kinds of practices, actors, and organizations are legitimate.[8] These beliefs promote the democratization of everyday life through demystification of professional authority combined with antielitism and are core ideals underlying self-help. They connect it with historical patterns typical of American antiauthoritarianism. Self-help relies on the experiential authority of its members and is radically democratic in promoting mutual trust and reciprocity among group members with a shared common condition. Recent theorizing about the public sphere (e.g., Cohen and Arato 1992), suggests that new social movements such as self-help represent post-1960s trends that promote the democratization of *all* institutions in civil society, not merely political ones.

Moreover, self-help groups and individuals often engage in explicit sociopolitical struggles. Not only does the National Alliance for the Mentally Ill provide a noninstitutionalized organizational setting that competes with state- and professionally-run mental health programs, but it actively engages in efforts to alter the legal conditions under which the provision of services is undertaken (Katz 1993). The National Sudden Infant Death Foundation conducts political campaigns involving the usual elements of social movements: mobilizing grievances among its constituency, tactical development, and managing institutional opposition (Bergman 1986). Naturally, different types of authorities in different arenas elicit a range of collective activity. Some responses may include creation of parallel sociopolitical structures, or pre-figurative spaces, characteristic of separatist wings of any number of left and right political movements. Due to the already marginalized nature of self-help members, an exit strategy aimed at creating parallel networks beyond manipulation of institutionalized healthcare seems to be a common tactic used in the self-help movement.

This suggests an important caveat with regard to the generality of processes involved in the evolution of self-help. My framework applies to certain kinds of social movement organizations that emphasize *personal transformation and transformation of social relationships* as a source of social and institutional change. These collectivities are explicitly new social movements. Other examples include religious movements, and groups within the gay rights and women's movements. Since health social movements that focus on the experience of illness, such as self-help, are contingent on a certain set of motivational assumptions, political movements dependent on other underlying assumptions do not share the same underlying explanations. That is, the question of personal motivation becomes salient for self-help (as for gay rights and women's groups) because it is likely that variation in motivations for participation differ from old-style political groups such as those found in the labor movement. Nonetheless, the organizations-social movement framework that I develop here, based on the spread of similar organizations and their practices, provides a broad enough conceptual umbrella as to apply to a number of diverse social movements and their organizations.

This umbrella conceptualizes social movements as collective challenges to constituted authority in nongovernmental institutional domains (e.g., Snow 2004; Cress and Myers 2004). I apply this idea to self-help in order to see how it is similar to and differs from movements challenging other institutional domains. As the studies in Myers and Cress (2004) make clear, this extension of the concept of social movement to include non-state-centered struggles is crucial to investigating the processes and mechanisms that shape movements and movement outcomes. Does this conceptualization readily apply to an organizational form that ranges widely from retreatist to politically engaged? I argue that we cannot know a priori that it does or not and therefore, the result is a rather unique application of an authority-in-contention framework to an organizational form that differs radically from old-style political social movement organizations. Surprisingly, some of its strategies for acquiring legitimacy are as politically centered as those used by, for example, labor or environmental movements, while other repertoires of action involve exit or separatist strategies (not unlike those of other identity movements). By extending the social movement framework, the generality of my explanations is broadened at the same time that this innovative organizational form becomes more comprehensible. One of the ways I do so is to examine how the movement is shaped internally by growth of its organizations, whose practices are initially independent of one another and then spread widely as other organizations mimic the practices of successful groups. Another way is to investigate how shifts in the broader culture facilitate growth of successful groups.

The Growth of Self-Help

Although a considerable amount of research on modern self-help as a cultural phenomenon has been undertaken during the last several decades (e.g., McGee 2005, Simonds 1992), studies of the growth of self-help have been limited. Most studies focus on the historical evolution of single groups, such as Alcoholics Anonymous (e.g., Makela 1996; Rudy and Greil 1988), Co-Dependents Anonymous (Rice 1996), or Depression After Delivery (Taylor 1996). Some work emphasizes the growth of groups connected to larger self-help organizations. For example, in Thomas J. Powell's (1994) compilation of current self-help research, Nash and Kramer (1994) describe a nationwide study of the groups comprising a self-help organization devoted to sickle-cell anemia. Yet, few provide comprehensive demographics of the movement. Those few demographic studies have yielded important insights but are limited to research of eighteen-month growth patterns among a small selection of self-help organizations in New Jersey in the early 1980s (Leventhal et al. 1988), a study of group fit (Maton 1989), a cross-sectional survey conducted in a couple of major U.S. cities (Davison, Pennebaker, and Dickerson 2000) and patterns of disbanding among 339 groups (Wituk et al. 2002), among others.

The question remains, what explains the growth of the movement? Some theoretically oriented research explores reasons for the emergence and institutionalization of self-help (very broadly construed). There are generally two varieties of this type of explanatory research. One takes a critical stance and focuses on how broad cultural patterns articulate with the self-help ethos. The analytic method usually focuses on a close textual reading of self-help books and programs that are hypothesized to reflect dominant cultural values such as asceticism, self-reliance, mental hygiene, and women's caretaking roles. These studies I refer to as ideological explanations because they are interested in why people believe the things they do and how this has led to a self-help movement. In some versions, the question is more narrowly focused on why women believe what they do and how this leads to their participation in self-help, through reading books or membership in support groups (e.g., Simonds 1992). The emphasis in these accounts of self-help is on the notion of the "self" and its beliefs, an individual-level characteristic that, while fashioned by social forces, remains isolated. Self-help becomes what it is in the ideological account because it is an expression of broader cultural beliefs that variously shape individuals and their social activities. For example, the twin ideals of success and self-invention, the self-made man, as it were, have a long pedigree as a literary genre from Franklin, Dale Carnegie, and Norman Vincent Peale to Steven Covey that articulates with the ethos of self-help (see McGee 2005). Contemporary self-help books, and support groups to a great extent, sustain the notion of reimagining the self as something different and better. While the specific language of self-invention in modern self-help differs from that of writers like Franklin, of course, the underlying principle of inventing oneself anew resonates with many a program aimed at individual transformation in the face of stigmatizing disability contained in self-help books. The other way of explaining self-help is more organizationally based. This type of study focuses on a single case of self-help organization or generic portrayals (but not analysis) of the self-help movement (usually defined as Alcoholics Anonymous). These approaches give rise to the thesis that "loss of traditional supports" creates the social necessity of self-help (see e.g., Smith and Pillemer

1983; Kauffman 1995). In line with this premise, self-help arises as a consequence of unmet social welfare and healthcare needs. Mental illness is one example. During the 1970s and 1980s, failure of mainstream healthcare to provide humane facilities for the mentally ill led to deinstitutionalization, and created a problematic situation for families of the mentally ill newly returned to their communities. Coalitions of these families formed the National Alliance for the Mentally Ill to solve personal and public problems generated by deinstitutionalization. Alcoholism is another example. The inability of mainstream social welfare and healthcare services to control alcohol and drug abuse led a number of individuals to create their own organizations devoted to solving this persistent social and personal ill. Research based on these and other similar cases argues that growth in self-help is a natural outcome of the continuing formation of groups to meet previously unmet needs (Katz 1993). The dynamic underlying this explanation is that localized problem-solving leads to the diffusion of self-help practices from mental health and addictions to other domains.

At the same time, social and political opportunities for group action aimed at resolving conflicts, a framework for presenting these issues, group identity and organizational structures for conducting ongoing campaigns to resolve grievances, are as essential for the growth of self-help as unmet needs. Although unmet needs are not irrelevant, for without grievances, people would not band together to solve their problems, the dilemma is that the self-help advocacy literature explains the rise of self-help based on the grievance argument almost exclusively. Like other individual-level explanations, this argument fails to connect with the fundamental issue of the organizational contexts in which mutual-aid occurs, collective action arises, and new group identities are shaped. Moreover, self-help research offers no comprehensive description of the processes by which the self-help *organizational form,* that is, the self-help movement, becomes institutionalized over the period of time between the end of World War II and the start of the twenty-first century. It is diffusion of the organizational form, and the dynamics of collective behavior reflected in self-help, that makes for its unique contribution to the burgeoning of complementary and alternative healthcare and captures our interest.

Why Study Self-Help Organizations?

There are a number of reasons to study self-help organizations. Sociological research could benefit immensely from close examination of the dynamics of a new associational form that, by all accounts, generates considerable social capital. Research on the internal dynamics of self-help shows that its groups are superior arenas for what social psychologists call cognitive restructuring and social reintegration (Rappaport 1993; Humphreys and Rappaport 1993; Humphreys and Kaskutas 1995). These processes take place because self-help serves as a normative, narrative community in which participants join their individual story to that of the community (Kurtz 1997). Community participation is facilitated by noncompetitiveness and cooperation, sustained by an egalitarian and tolerant ideology where norms of reciprocity operate. Moreover, membership and participation in self-help fosters trust, cooperation, and mutualism, all key elements of social capital. In addition, self-help creates new categories of people such as the recovering addict and new activities such as the ritualistic sharing of stories (see Humphreys and Rappaport 1993). If self-help advocates' case descriptions were not enough to convince us that self-help produces new identities, consider that critics of women's participation in self-help such as Simonds (1992) and Rapping (1996) are fiercely antagonistic to the idea of self-help's construction of the "woman in recovery," whose new identity, it is argued by these critics, supersedes her identity as a socially and politically progressive woman.

On a wider scale, self-help organizations enrich society by fostering a new way of problem-solving, which translates into a new means of self-governance. Internal processes become encoded in the structure of the self-help organization in the form of programs and routines linking members to larger social structures. Support groups (Wuthnow 1994:360):

> bring a personal human dimension to public life. They allow people to be themselves, to be vulnerable, to be weak, to be emotionally distraught, to be recovering from addictions, and yet to participate in the collective life of our society.

Another reason to pursue the study of self-help organizations is that the growth of a diverse, independent health and human services organizational sector, spurred on by self-help, suggests widespread change in the area of social participation and institution-building at odds with the decline-of-civil-society thesis. Putnam (2000) argues that one of the clearest exceptions to civic disengagement includes the increase in self-help support groups. Despite this claim, because of the lack of empirical research on self-help dynamics, it remains unclear how, where, and why this increase in self-help support groups has occurred. Putnam derives his claim from the observations of Katz (1993), Riessman and Carroll (1995), Lieberman and Snowden (1994), and other advocates who make arguments about self-help growth based on clinical rather than epidemiological research. In contrast, Chapter Three demonstrates that the decline of self-help founding rates had already begun by the time Putnam and others (e.g., Katz 1993) announced the burgeoning of self-help, around the mid-1980s. The decline in founding rates combined with accelerated dissolution rates, led to an overall decrease in the size of the organizational population by the early 1990s. Were there, thus, fewer groups for a declining pool of constituents or fewer groups but a still-growing pool of constituents? Although we cannot answer the question completely, because no one has any reliable participation figures at this point, we do know that there was a decline in the number of self-help organizations formed and a slight increase in rates at which already formed groups dissolved by the late 1990s. This decline in self-help organizations suggests that growth of the movement had stabilized, either because more groups disbanded or participation dropped or both (Wituk et al. 2002).

But why should scholars, self-help members, and practitioners be interested in how the self-help *organizational population* changes? One useful way to answer the question from an organizational perspective is to consider that organizations are central actors in modern societies. Populations of organizations are repositories of collective knowledge about how to accomplish collective tasks. The "ability of society as a whole to respond to changing conditions depends on the responsiveness of its constituent organizations and on the diversity of its organizational populations" (Hannan and Freeman 1989:3). Therefore, the study of organizations holds considerable importance for several reasons. Organizations provide the context for a variety of general social processes including socialization, interpersonal communication, goal and status attainment, institutionalization, and stratification (Scott 2003). They also provide a distinctive setting that differentially affects how these fundamental social processes are carried out. In addition, organizations reflect societal conditions and affect social structure outside of organizations; they institutionalize beliefs and practices, and serve as templates for future collective action. Most importantly, organizations exist as collective actors in their own right, shaping social, economic, and political arenas.

As I have argued, self-help is fundamentally an organizational phenomenon, and self-help research has an implicit interest in diversity in organizational populations. To understand self-help, it is particularly important to conduct a systematic survey of changes in the shape of the movement and the sources promoting its institutionalization. That is, lacking self-help demographic data, no research addresses the basic issue of how self-help organizational forms are reproduced and evolve over time, and while some offer general descriptions of the processes by which self-help becomes popular, none provide systematic observations of all organizations over time. To address this issue I examine the diffusion of self-help organizations, their struggles, alliances and compromises with authorities, and competition among them. Some useful questions that drive this research are therefore: What are the dynamics of self-help and what social forces influence these dynamics? Explaining the dynamics of organizational populations is the goal of organizational ecology, which, when combined with an institutional framework rooted in social movements (see Campbell 2005; Schneiberg and Soule 2005) provides a larger perspective for understanding the growth of organizational populations.

An Organizational Ecology of Health Movement Organizations

Organizational ecology is the study of organizational emergence, growth and dissolution through application of a biological, natural selection model to organizations. Organizational ecologists are interested in the diversity of organizational forms (e.g., an HMO, a drug treatment facility, or a self-help group) and focus on populations of similar organizations in order to understand how changes take place over extended periods of time (Scott 2003). Organizational ecologists analyze organizational populations because the emergence of a new population of organizations or the creation of a new ecological niche through expansion of an organizational population influences social, economic, and political structures throughout the social system. Changes in social structure influence the diversity of organizations and the emergence of new kinds of organizations requires a new community of sustaining organizations, and comparable supporting financial, social, and political arrangements (Scott 2003). Each of these new organizational populations arises as a result of selection processes.

Selection processes cause new organizational forms to emerge and disappear, and are empirically represented by organizational founding and dissolution rates. One advantage of studying organizational vital rates is that the dynamics of organizational formation and dissolution allow us to specify concretely how organizational environments shape the emergence, decline, and persistence of new forms for almost all forms of organization (Carroll and Hannan 2000). Legitimation (public recognition) and competition (for material resources) are two key processes known to be instrumental in the growth and decline of many organizational populations and are core processes by which institutionalization takes place. The prevalence of an organizational form suggests that legitimation processes are at work, since legitimation, in the form of acceptance and taken-for-grantedness, grows along with the increasing number of organizations in the population. As a consequence, organizational founding rates rise and failure rates decline, perpetuating the growth of the population overall. However, as organizations gain acceptance, become taken for granted, and proliferate, competition for finite resources of the organizational niche increases markedly. As the effects of legitimation processes stabilize, competition intensifies and erodes the gains made by legitimation, slowing organizational formation considerably, since organizers will have access to fewer resources with which to found new organizations. Resources also decline for already existing organizations such that organizational dissolutions begin to accelerate relative to organizational foundings, and the size of the population shrinks. This trajectory may reach a steady state so that foundings and dissolutions become relatively balanced.

Organizational ecology, because of its explanatory generality, has been applied to an astonishing range of organizational populations from newspapers, insurances companies, and breweries to social service agencies, unions, and the women's movement (see Carroll and Hannan 2000 for review). It helps us understand one road by which the phenomena represented by these populations (e.g., women's issues, social services in Canada, breweries in the United States) become institutionalized. Still, its generality becomes a liability unless the specific historical contexts of the cases are spelled out.

Legitimation, Competition, and Self-Help

Why are legitimation and competition processes important in shaping self-help? Legitimation processes are essential for organizational viability because legitimate organizations attract a broader constituency and gain better access to economic and political resources. Self-help organizations seek legitimacy and as organizational legitimacy diffuses from one organization to the next the size of the population grows. The emergence of Adult Children of Alcoholics (ACoA) and Co-Dependents Anonymous (CoDA) provides a useful illustration of how self-help thrives on the burgeoning of its legitimacy in the various arenas of medicine, academia, popular culture, and politics.

Adult Children of Alcoholics and Co-Dependents Anonymous are organizations devoted to the so-called illness of co-dependency. Presenting complaints include a series of psychological problems, ranging from anxiety and depression to compulsive and addictive behavior. ACoA was founded in New York in 1970, and nationwide in 1977. It was an offshoot of the two main groups, Al-Anon and Alateen, which addressed issues of co-dependency in relationships with alcoholics and drug addicts (Katz 1993). ACoA arose from philosophical differences with its mother organization, Al-Anon World Services, concerning the nature of recovery in co-dependent relationships with addicts (Rice 1996). In 1979, *Newsweek* published a story about several prominent co-dependency proponents (i.e., Claudia Black, Stephanie Brown, Sharon Wegschieder-Cruse) and in 1982 a psychologist, Janet G. Woititz, published *Adult Children of Alcoholics*. A few years later, Jael Greenleaf's (1987) *Co-Alcoholic, Para-Alcoholic: Who's Who and What's the Difference?* came out along with a number of articles and books referencing co-dependency such as Sharon Wegschieder-Cruse (1984) *Co-Dependency: An Emerging Issue*; Melodie Beattie (1987) *Co-Dependent No More: How to Stop Controlling Others and Care for Yourself*; Anne Wilson Schaeff (1986) *Co-Dependence- Misunderstood-Mistreated*; Anne Wilson Schaeff (1987) *When Society Becomes an Addict*; and John Bradshaw (1988) *Bradshaw on the Family*. These articles and books explained the basic ideas of co-dependency, helped ACoA and CoDA recruit new members, and doubled the actual number of national organizations addressing co-dependency.

But there can be only so many organizations addressing the issue of co-dependency since the supply of members and resources to run the organizations is limited (just as it is limited in commercial sectors). Competition for resources therefore structures the growth of the population in important ways. Despite uncertainty about the extent to which competitive forces operate in nonprofit sectors (Knoke 1986, 1989), researchers generally agree that nonprofit organizations engage in competition for resources, status and clients (see e.g., Baum and Oliver 1996; Popielarz and McPherson 1995). One way to conceptualize competition between voluntary associations is in terms of resource overlap. Resource overlap occurs when self-help organizations share a finite resource base consisting of services, membership, and social technologies (i.e., programs, ideologies, and organizational procedures). From the 1970s through the 1990s a number of self-help organizations arose with overlapping specialty areas. Organizational resources diminished by overlap might involve physical space for meetings, trained volunteers, or the availability of constituencies to join multiple organizations. To the extent that an organization is able to offer unique services it will survive longer than organizations that cannot do so. Both the ACoA and CoDA, for instance, meet in a public space, such as a church, public library, or hospital conference room. In this regard, they draw on finite resources and therefore compete with each other and other organizations dependent on the church or hospital for free or inexpensive meeting space. When organizations vie for resources to provide the same service—such as nutritional programs, childcare, and transportation—resource overlap increases, competition rises, and the pool of resources declines. Sooner or later, one of these organizations will disband. And as more organizations disband, resources become available for surviving organizations and for new ones. Competition thus follows legitimation as one of the two crucial mechanisms by which institutional-building takes place. Together they create the ideological and material openings in public space through which self-help becomes an institution.

How a Health Movement Became an Institution: Institutionalism and New Social Movements

Social institutions like medicine, science, and constitutional government act as the rules of the game (North 1990), articulating with the practices of organizations. Institutions entail normative rules—informally and formally prescribed standards of behavior and practice—which enter into social life as facts. The processes of institutionalization involve the activities and mechanisms by which practices, structures, and behaviors like self-help become taken for granted society-wide. Institutionalized behavior is taken for granted because of the unquestioning acceptance and conformity found among people who practice it.[9] When there is a need to explain or legitimate action, institutions carry their own rationales. These are "logics" or ideologies and they might be rank-ordered from primary ones to secondary ones depending on their use to justify behavior. Self-reliance might be one such logic that fits into a larger pattern of antielitism and leads groups to try and democratize spheres of everyday life, perhaps beginning with group decision-making processes themselves.

The dynamics by which social behavior becomes taken for granted are complex and one of the chief questions underlying social science investigation. Some researchers see organizations, including social movements, as the starting point of institutionalization and others see institutionalization processes occurring first at the societal or cultural level. Schneiberg and Soule (2005) describe a number of different theoretical perspectives on institutional processes, and emphasize how these might be applied to social movements. I detail this framework in Chapter Two but I introduce it here to explain the notion of institution-building in self-help.

Social practices become taken for granted as a result of cultural expression (or enactment) of some larger symbolic entity, they can result from diffusion of practices at a local level, or they may emerge from political contests over control of a jurisdiction. One set of explanations for self-help envisions a top-down process whereby broad cultural patterns in beliefs and behavior about how and why societies are ordered and organized the way they are, sustained self-help practices. Studies of self-help often allude to the ideals of ascetic Protestantism, which generates movement values associated with the practice of utilitarianism and individualism (e.g., returning the locus of control from doctors to individual patients).

Another set of explanations claims that self-help springs from unmet needs. Innovation in a practice or behavior occurs in response to unmet needs, which is then adopted by other individual actors at the local level. Other actors (e.g., movement organizers) then imitate the innovators and the innovation spreads throughout the field. Legitimacy follows from conformity to spread of the practice, even when the practice does not meet the specific needs of adopters. For example, the program of Alcoholics Anonymous (AA) (1935) became the basis for all of the other anonymous groups including those that might have used other methods for dealing with their focal problem (e.g., eating disorders, sexual dysfunction). The key mechanism in this model is that as the number of adopters increases, relevant authorities endorse innovation, which gains legitimacy and becomes the norm. Soon it is adopted by others unthinkingly. This explains the wide diversity in what constitutes self-help, from addiction to cancer groups.

In the chapters to follow, we will see how physicians and other medical professionals who support the development of alternative practices such as self-help are central to legitimation. This suggests another important route to institutionalization. Sociopolitical struggles over jurisdiction are a critical source of institution building. They work very simply: conflict between local actors, over for instance the delivery of addiction treatment, creates legitimation crises, established forms of treatment become suspect, and their taken-for-grantedness disappears (Stryker 2000). Later, struggles end in victory or compromise, political reconstruction occurs and institutionalization of new practices takes place. In the self-help literature, the issue of sociopolitical struggles is paramount because self-help is a preeminent challenger to institutionalized healthcare and it faces a number of problems in the process of diffusion that mainstream actors engaged in political contests do not. For instance, how do challenger organizations in healthcare, such as self-help, acquire necessary professional legitimacy from medical authorities when these sources represent their antagonists? In a very important sense, as much as self-help became a *popularly* recognized, taken-for-granted set of beliefs and practices, it is still contested by mainstream health practitioners and as such must continually struggle to assert its status as a legitimate healthcare service. It might be argued that this does not count as taken-for-grantedness. But practices are not either all legitimated or not, nor is there ever a single audience by which institutionalization is solely determined. Some practices may achieve relative institutional status in one area while requiring ongoing social movement support to sustain them in other areas (Polletta 2004; but cf. Jepperson 1991).

Within this enactment-diffusion-politics framework we can see how the three processes foster the conditions under which self-help emerges and becomes institutionalized. The model creates the link between the mechanisms of legitimation and competition and the demographics of the self-help population because it allows us to make comparisons between organizations over the course of the population's history that address fundamental issues (like political contests) in movement evolution. The following chapters provide a portrait of the evolution of this population and reveal that while self-help is as different from conventional healthcare as other complementary and alternative practices, the basic patterns of population change from emergence through maturity leading to institutionalization depend on how organizers acquire legitimacy and handle competition. To make the link clear, Chapter Two begins with some basic concepts. I start by defining self-help as an organizational phenomenon. From this definition cases are amassed and the creation of a longitudinal database undertaken. The dataset captures the total self-help population of 589 national organizations and features information on the attributes of these organizations that are used for analyzing the evolution of this population of organizations, including its sources of legitimation and competition. I then discuss how most of the research in self-help has focused not on the demographics of its organizations but on its ideological underpinnings and show that while this is important information explaining why self-help might exist, it does not explain how it becomes taken for granted (i.e., how this social movement became a social institution). Using Schneiberg and Soule (2005) I discuss how an organizations-social movement framework helps us understand the process of institution-building in self-help.

Chapter Three provides researchers with a description of the central patterns of growth, decline, and longevity of the self-help population of organizations. The first section of this chapter discusses the primary sources of data for this study of self-help and then provides a brief theoretical background for understanding the patterns in the tables that follow. The second section describes the actual patterns of organizational growth, decline, and longevity in the self-help population. The third section of this chapter analyzes resource partitioning—cultivation of special resource niches in mature populations (Carroll and Hannan 2000)—in the self-help population by showing how specialists and generalists in eighteen subpopulations in the sector gain market share—the proportion of the total available self-help "market" or membership. The underlying question concerning the extent to which legitimation and competition play a role in growth and diversification lays the groundwork for later chapters.

Chapter Four examines how legitimation processes unfold in a discussion of several exemplary cases, drawing attention to the contrast between how self-help seeks institutional support from entrenched interests while retaining an ethos of opposition to mainstream healthcare. Here individual members of self-help describe how self-help became legitimate. The central theme is that self-help organizations face challenges in achieving public recognition from medical, academic, popular, and political sources that they must overcome in order to survive. To the extent that individual organizations can do so, the movement thrives.

Chapter Five draws out the unique contributions medical, academic, popular, and political legitimation make to the different kinds of self-help groups. The central premise is that diffusion of self-help fosters legitimacy that differentially affects groups. Institutionalization results from growing legitimation. Three central questions motivate the discussion in this chapter. Are some sources of legitimation more important than others? Do these have differential effects on different types of self-help organizations—how long do they last? And how does differential recognition affect their formation?

Chapter Six details struggles between groups over scarce resources. Legitimation promotes self-help and competition selects the fittest organizations for survival, causing others to disband. Just as Chapter Five mapped the growth of self-help through examination of the effects of legitimation on organizational formation, Chapter Six captures the dynamics of competition by examining the rate at which organizations dissolve. As in the previous chapter, three central questions motivate the discussion in this chapter. What are the long-term trends in competition among self-help organizations? How does competition unfold among the different types of self-help organizations? And how does competition differentially affect the dissolution of medical, behavioral, psychological, and general groups?

Chapter Seven recapitulates the argument that the process of institutionalization entails, first, the growth and diversification of self-help which, next, garners legitimacy and fosters its acceptance as a new social institution while, lastly, generating competition that helps solidify population gains through selecting only the fittest organizations. Having shown this through empirical analysis of self-help organizational data, I draw implications for the continued consolidation of self-help as well as implications for the growth of health social movements in general. For instance, science and medicine are sources of authority. A good deal of this power lies in the connection between science, medicine, and the political economy. To the extent that health social movements specifically challenge institutionalized healthcare, they can bring about change in the political economy (Zavestoski et al. 2004).

In this chapter I include several limitations of the study and propose additional research questions that might fill in gaps, given these analyses, such as: what social and cultural factors other that legitimation and resource use shape alternative healthcare practices and do these extend to other health movements such as breast cancer, AIDS and urban anti-drug movements? An apt use of the research in this book would be to extend research on institutionalization to exploration of the influence of health movements such as these on changes in institutional healthcare in the United States and elsewhere. For example, the recovery movement has brought about the widespread use of the twelve-step program of the anonymous groups in formal clinical settings. How does this happen and what are the institutional forces that influence this process? A larger project could use the evolution of self-help as the anchor to explain how social movement organizations shape and are shaped by healthcare institutions. In an important sense, the study of diverse health movement populations provides a context for understanding how different organizational forms signal shifts in the composition of different versions of civil society, and the role organizational dynamics play in expansion of this sphere: an ongoing expansion for over the past hundred years in this country, and one just beginning in many others. The lessons learned here will therefore be all the more important for the future development of societies, including our own, that are now witnessing dramatic changes in their civil institutions.

2

Defining Self-Help: How Does a Movement Become an Institution?

What is self-help and how do researchers define it? One of the barriers to understanding self-help is that "self-help" refers to a broad and confusing array of phenomena ranging from books and programs to cultural trends (Riessman 1985). In contrast to an encompassing definition, the more manageable definition of self-help in this book focuses on the psychotherapeutic support groups and organizations that constitute it (Borkman 1991; Schubert and Borkman 1991). Self-help organizations are formal structures that are sustained by a differentiated, complex, organizational structure consisting of groups, meetings, chapters, boards, volunteers, staff, and affiliated networks (Powell 1990). The support group component, by which self-help is largely known beyond self-help books, addresses personal conditions ranging from medical disability to behavioral dysfunction. In this group space, members engage in psychotherapeutically oriented discussion. Stigmatizing conditions might cover healthcare issues such as amputation (National Amputee Foundation), alcoholism (Alcoholics Anonymous), an autistic child (Autism Network), or a relative with Alzheimer's Disease (Alzheimer's Disease and Related Disorders Association) as well as psychological problems associated with divorce, adoption or sexual orientation. One of the definitive aspects of self-help is that its support groups are organized and controlled by constituents whose problem or illness group processes are intended to address (Borkman 1999; Katz 1993; Kurtz 1999).

I start with a general definition of self-help that facilitates constructing a set of cases, detailed in the next chapter that can be used to analyze the evolution of this population of organizations, its sources of legitimation, and resource use. Then I discuss a theoretical frame-work for understanding how legitimation and resource use are core processes facilitating institutionalization. The main claim is that self-help functions as a challenger movement whose practices become nor-mative following recognition by authorities in medical, academic, political, and popular arenas.

Katz and Bender (1976:270–271), define self-help as:

> [s]mall group structures for mutual aid and the accomplishment of a special purpose. They are usually formed by peers who have come together for mutual assistance in satisfying a common need, overcom-ing a common handicap or life-disrupting problem, and bringing about desired social and/or personal change. The initiators and members of such groups perceive that their needs are not, or cannot be met by or through existing social institutions. Self-help groups emphasize face-to-face social interactions and the assumption of personal responsibil-ity by members. They often provide material assistance, as well as emotional support; they are frequently "cause" oriented, and promul-gate an ideology or values through which members may attain an enhanced sense of personal identity.

These small group structures are (U.S. Department of Health and Human Services 1987):

> self-governing groups whose members share a common concern and give each other emotional support and material aid, charge either no fee or only a small fee for membership, and place a high value on expe-riential knowledge in the belief that it provides special understanding of a situation. In addition to providing mutual support for their mem-bers, such groups may also be involved in information, education, material aid, and social advocacy in their communities.

Critical elements of these groups entail: a common problem that allows members to identify with one another and facilitates cognitive restructuring; the helper principle in which the helper is helped by helping others; a support network through which group members provide social, emotional, and sometimes material support via meet-ings, telephone calls, newsletters, conferences, and nowadays, the Internet; shared information, so that knowledge is produced and exchanged within the organization; nominal or nonexistent costs; unconditional love that involves the nonjudgmental acceptance of others in the group; and equality among members based on experience of the personal stigmatizing condition or problem (Hedrick, Isenberg, and Martini 1992).

In short, self-help promotes a philosophy of self-determination based on an intimate, experiential understanding of the focal problem of the group. Membership is often (though not always) limited to those who experience some kind of physical or psychological condition of a stigmatizing or marginalizing nature, or who are related to those who do. As researchers who study sickness and health note, mental and physical crises throw people out of their ordinary lives, and illness erodes the taken-for-granted continuity in life. Having lost the taken-for-grantedness of sound body and mind, people who have a chronic illness, or are associated with those who do, often experience the loss as insurmountable. The Alliance for Lung Cancer Advocacy is a good example of a group of patients (including their families and friends) who have been treated for a disease that carries a special stigma because of its association with cigarette smoking. Members are cancer patients whose social standing as people with a putatively self-induced fatal illness makes them vulnerable to negative social sanctions of varying degrees (Charmaz 2000). If nothing else, they are shunned as being physically impaired and less able to carry out their normal social roles (Goffman 1963). The Alliance provides a re-integrative context by means of moral and material support through discussion and information exchange about the nature of the disease among those who are undergoing or have undergone treatment.

As for non-patient members, professionals and other interested groups can be provisional members of self-help organizations. However, as long as their interests remain professional, membership is problematic. To clarify the relationship among professionals and group members, it is important to distinguish between several types of groups engaged in therapeutic activities, only one of which is self-help in its ideal form.

Support Groups, Psychotherapy Groups, and Professional Involvement

Self-help organizations, support groups, and psychotherapy groups represent different group-therapeutic solutions to individual problems (Kurtz 1997). Support groups and psychotherapy groups are arranged for similar purposes under the auspices of a social service agency or formally organized healthcare organization. These groups emphasize external actions on behalf of an individual or individuals while self-help in the "best American tradition" involves "individuals who all exhibit initiative on their own behalf...but act in tandem to assure greater benefits" (Bartalos 1992:71). The chief difference between the three types of groups lies in the use of professionals. Self-help is least likely to use professionals as group leaders or moderators and it is distinguished from other group therapeutic activities insofar as it is always member-centered, even when professional moderators are invited to participate. For self-help groups, professionals may act as consultants. They can provide referrals, serve as a speaker or coleader, and connect the group to external resources. Where professionals are group leaders, the principle of self-help is largely violated. Use of professional leaders or moderators tends to introduce the payment of fees, limitations on group membership, introduction of complex therapeutic methods, creation of distance and hierarchy between professionals and group members, and dependence on extra-organizational resources for survival (Kurtz 1997). However, a group in which the "professional has the role of facilitator or resource person and decisions are actually thrashed out by and within the group," constitutes genuine self-help (Kurtz 1997:159). Many groups need the guidance and help provided by professionals.

Several examples serve to highlight the professional's role in self-help. Parents Anonymous is a self-help organization devoted to prevention of child abuse and it uses volunteer professional facilitators such as social workers, teachers, heathcare givers, pastoral counselors, and student interns. First Sunday is a group of couples who have lost a child. The group is facilitated by psychiatric social workers, clergy, and physicians but the group's focus is on couples who share their experiences of loss with each other. Another example, The National Alliance for the Mentally Ill (NAMI), uses professional consultants on its national board of directors, although only patients and their families are eligible to serve in the leadership structure of NAMI. Other groups with professional connections include the Candlelighters Childhood Cancer Foundation, Alzheimer's Disease and Related Disorders, and The Compassionate Friends (grief support following death of a child).

The incorporation of professionals into self-help introduces potential for conflict. Struggles over who gets to be involved in self-help, and how this involvement is linked to other areas of institutional activity (such as professional and state control), is important for an understanding of the extent to which self-help functions as a legitimate alternative to mainstream healthcare. Lee and Swenson (1994:422) note that "implicit in the self-help concept is a re-evaluation of professional helping" and a critique of existing institutions that challenges the value and role of professionals. As I discuss later, this critical stance forces self-help outside of mainstream healthcare and makes borrowing from already legitimated practices of practitioners challenging. From the point of view of medical professionals, self-help is suspect for a number of reasons: nonprofessionally led groups may give erroneous information, bad advice, and inadequate therapeutic support to members; the exchange of intense feelings may cause extreme distress to other group members; irregular attendance creates instability in groups and fosters individual distrust and maladjustment; groups for people with fatal medical conditions can be detrimental for members in different stages of terminal illness; and groups "may pressure newcomers to accept stigmatized identities and cult-like beliefs" whether or not they actually identify with other group members (Bartalos 1992:31). In short, these problems set the stage for conflict over the practice of healthcare. Conflict takes place between medical professionals and local and national organizations, and involves the core activities of self-help groups.

Voluntary Associations and Self-Help Organizations

Self-help is a type of voluntary association that differs from social service groups, political advocacy groups, mutual aid societies (which cover labor unions, professional associations, mutual benefit associations, and friendly societies), and self-improvement groups. It differs from groups that engage in political change activities, such as a neighborhood watch association or a chapter of the Green Party in terms of outcomes, goals, and strategies. These kinds of organizations tend to have an instrumental focus, largely aimed at the political system while self-help does not. Rather, self-help groups closely resemble mutual-aid societies in that "members of the group expend substantial effort in their roles as group members trying to improve the situation and quality of life of other members" (Smith and Pillemer 1983:204). However, this might be said of "labor unions, employers' associations, community associations, taxpayers' associations, producer and consumer cooperatives" as well (p.204). Self-help groups, unlike mutual aid groups, focus on trying to improve group members' personal problems utilizing therapeutic or curative group activities. While mutual aid is a necessary defining characteristic of self-help, self-help groups are unique in that members perceive the group as a chance to ameliorate a pressing personal problem "that directly affects the individual participant whether or not any other individuals suffer from it" (p.205). This part of the definition excludes social service and professional providers who might organize and advocate for patients' rights. Furthermore, self-help groups differ from self-improvement groups such as Great Books Discussion Groups and Toastmasters groups in that members of these groups do not suffer from any immediate disadvantage. Self-help groups also differ from group psychotherapy and human potential groups (e.g., Erhard Seminars Training (EST), sensitivity training, encounter groups) because they are oriented to reconstruction of stigmatized identities (a public project) rather than simple psychological reconstruction. In addition, what makes self-help unique is that unlike other organizational forms, the span of control for self-help organizations is strictly egalitarian.

In this study, I focus on national self-help organizations. Self-help functions as a federation of local autonomous units with broad decision-making powers and a wide geographic dispersion of national self-help organizations. National self-help organizations consist of local groups. The cornerstone, for instance, of Alcoholics Anonymous, one of self-help's oldest organizations, is the local AA group (Kurtz 1979) found in virtually every community in the United States, and in most foreign countries as well (AA World Services 2005). These local groups, in one sense, *are* Alcoholics Anonymous, just as the local chapter of Self-Help for the Hard of Hearing is Self-Help for the Hard of Hearing. Self-help grows from the bottom up, usually with only a handful of individual members to begin with. Later it develops an increasing division of labor as membership grows and groups spring up everywhere. Having done so, self-help organizations establish organizational routines and structures within their broad-based membership. If they desire, they then become a national presence in order to reach as many potential members as possible.

To chronicle the processes of growth, decline, diversification, and resource partitioning, and to describe how self-help attains legitimacy and institutional standing, I let national self-help organizations represent self-help.[1] National self-help organizations are long-lasting and offer well-developed support programs among local chapters, meetings, and groups. They provide stability and predictability, and have a more diverse membership and a stronger leadership structure than fragmented or unaffiliated groups (Powell 1987, 1990). Well-developed programs for supporting members depend on a comprehensive organizational structure tightly linked to the goals of mutual aid.

A comprehensive system of norms and procedures limits disruptive behavior, fosters community, reduces individual differences, and promotes personal growth. Given the often chaotic mental state in which an individual, driven to a self-help group, finds himself or herself, organizational stability and predictably are preconditions that mitigate the detrimental effects of illness and disease. This facilitates the process of recovery through conversation that is at the core of the social technology of the self-help group.

The most important caveat in this study is that this is not a study about self-help *groups* per se, except insofar as self-help organizations consist of groups. It is, however, an analysis of the dynamic processes by which the *population* of self-help organizations grows, which is based on the premise of group expansion. Sometimes the discussion conflates organizations and groups because self-help organizations consist of self-help groups or they would not be self-help organizations in the way that I am defining them.

Nonetheless, not all self-help groups are formal organizations with established structures (e.g., chairpersons, treasurers, secretaries, and so forth). Some are informal and emerge and fade away rapidly, which is the reason I do not analyze self-help groups, just national organizations. This has implications for legitimation since national self-help organizations have probably acquired a measure of recognition that informal groups operating out of someone's living room have not. To analyze the self-help movement using a demographic model necessitates the use of "long- lived" organizations, at least those with enough formal structure to sustain them one year. In constructing a dataset for analysis of population demographics, only organizations that define themselves as national self-help organizations are included. And yet some of these, such as Wegener's Granulomatosis, are not sizable formal organizations like Mended Hearts or Alcoholics Anonymous but small local organizations with a handful of members who call themselves a national organization in order to mobilize supporters. Over time, more groups resort to this strategy so that many national self-help organizations arise locally with already established formal structures in place.

Self-Help as a Population of Health Movement Organizations

Labeling self-help a social movement—challengers of the political status quo (Marx and McAdam 1994)—or even a health movement is not uncontroversial. Most researchers and practitioners tend to think of self-help groups and organizations as largely apolitical, disqualifying them as social movements. Katz' (1993) seminal work, *Self-Help in America: A Social Movement Perspective*, concludes that self-help has social movement-like features but strays from conventional definitions because there is no common political goal around which to rally supporters. Smith and Pillemer (1983) conclude that self-help is a social movement because self-help groups "seek change in both the informal support system of stigmatized individuals and in the relationship of such individuals to relevant human service professionals and institutions" (p.228). Makela (1996) uses a social movement framework to understand Alcoholics Anonymous, arguably one of the most apolitical, retreatist self-help organizations. He focuses on the differences between old-style political movements and new social movements. New social movements involve collective action that is oriented toward social and cultural change like other social movements but emphasizes the importance of how the (collective) identity of the participants unfolds in the activities of the movement, rather than simply focusing on the rational, goal-seeking behavior of participants. The difference between interest-based and new identity-based movements is that interest-based movements derive their legitimacy by striving to monopolize representation of constituencies and extending *rights* to constituents. Identity-based movements derive their legitimacy "by persuading others that they are authentically expressing the identity of particular subgroups while at the same time successfully signaling membership in the larger identity group" (Armstrong 2002:372). Broadening forms of possible self-expression is one of the benefits identity politics brings to its constituency. Health social movements are a good example. They 1) base their legitimacy on the experiences of those with the disease; 2) challenge healthcare practices and knowledge; and 3) offer collaborative opportunities to establish alternatives (Brown et al. 2004). To facilitate identity formation, health movements rearrange already familiar practices and established ways of operating, along with rationales explaining these new arrangements, and apply these to new enterprises. One strategic problem is how to extend accepted practices in one area of social life to another. Ideologues accomplish this by framing the new movement in terms of already familiar ways of engaging in collective activity.

Self-help advocates have been able to do so either consciously or unconsciously by tapping into other contemporary movements. Movements influence one another by altering the political and cultural environment so that advantages gained by one movement spill over to others (Meyer and Whittier 1994). They also influence actors within and between movements. Self-help as we know it today emerged contemporaneously with social practices such as women's consciousness raising, group psychotherapy, consumer rights, community-based health and human services, and new age religion during the transformation of the healthcare industry in the United States in 1960s and 1970s. It borrows the technologies and worldviews of these disparate forms and mobilizes around social, political, and personal change.

The diverse components of the movement include ideologies and programs (some promoted through self-help books), tertiary movements (e.g., the recovery movement, the twelve-step movement), social movement-like organizations and movement-affiliated organizations (Kriesi 1996), support groups, movement organizers and activists, and networks of constituents and members. Its main feature as a health movement is that it strives for formal and informal change in healthcare systems by engaging authority in multiple arenas, broadly construed. It provides a well-known set of alternative beliefs and practices, and fosters a new social identity linked to membership in the movement.

But is self-help a *health* movement? Although many self-help organizations deal with physical disability and illness, calling self-help a health movement is not uncontroversial since groups dealing with divorce, adoption, and being gay do not seem to address health issues per se. Yet, these stigmatized statuses generate huge amounts of psychological distress that their bearers are at pains to negotiate. Moreover, it is the technology of self-help, its psychosocial support groups, oriented toward restoring psychological well-being, that serves as the definitive characteristic of self-help as a *health* movement.

Self-help challenges institutionalized healthcare, which it views as insufficient to meet the needs of most people (Riessman and Carroll 1995). Self-help organizations bring about change in the healthcare sector by resisting the dominance of mainstream authorities, altering legal systems, and providing access to alternative healthcare resources. Self-help advocates also mobilize constituents, garner funds for research, challenge regulations and laws, and foster public discussion about the social conditions underlying their problems. The National Sudden Infant Death Syndrome Foundation is one such organization. It emerged in response to the mystery surrounding infant crib deaths and lack of medical information about causes and solutions. This organization was able to secure medical recognition and to advance its political agenda by translating medical legitimation into political capital. It became an important player in formulating legislation that resulted in the 1974 SIDS Act. Other organizations such as the National Alliance for the Mentally Ill, and even Alcoholics Anonymous, an organization known to abjure explicit political action, have been instrumental in sociopolitical changes in distribution of resources. For instance, Mary Mann, a member of AA and an alcoholism organizer, founded the National Council on Alcohol, while Senator Harold E. Hughes (another group member) played a pivotal role in establishing the National Institute of Alcoholism and Alcohol Abuse under the auspices of the Hughes Act in 1970.

Self-help functions as a challenger movement in other ways. In reaction to institutionalized healthcare, self-help constituents design their own healthcare systems in the form of self-help groups (Borkman 1991; Katz 1993; Powell 1994; Riessman and Carroll 1995). Anyone can form a self-help group, recruit members, and develop a program of psychotherapeutic support aimed at some focal condition or illness, such as cancer, infant death, depression, adoption, divorce, addiction, or heart disease, without professional credentials of any sort. This do-it-yourself method of healthcare has a cultural resonance for most Americans since its frame of reference depends on a history of self-sufficiency as well as an ideology of mutual assistance. De Tocqueville (1951 [1835]) observed this behavior a century and a half ago, remarking that Americans took it upon themselves to form small groups to pursue any and all issues from the weightiest public matter to the most trivial. The object of de Tocqueville's insight was the nineteenth-century version of contemporary self-help, the temperance movement, through which the private tragedy of inebriety and drunkenness was transformed into a public health issue, much to de Tocqueville's amazement. In France, these issues were addressed by government ministries, not by sociopolitical interest groups.

In attempting to understand how self-help evolved into the well-known phenomenon it is today, it is useful to keep in mind Borkman's (1999) nomenclature, which refers to self-help as *self-help/mutual aid*. Self-help is mutual aid because the crucial activity of self-help, what I refer to as the social technology of self-help, is reciprocal face-to-face psychosocial support that takes place within a group context. Although self-help encompasses a range of phenomena, it would cease to exist without the support groups that organize its primary activities. The salient principle of the group is that people who have a "common predicament or illness come together to provide emotional and other support through sharing their personal lived experiences as well as exchanging other resources" (Borkman 1991:644). Group-level processes foster an identity consistent with the movement's three central precepts: disenchantment with medicine, search for self-control and empowerment, and a holistic approach to health (Ruggie 2004).[2] As in other movements, the process of identity creation is one of conversion and involves biographical reconstruction in which a spoiled identity, such as being deaf, is converted into a socially acceptable one, such as being hearing-impaired. In this sense, self-help is probably more self-conscious in its reprogramming than other new social movements, such as gay rights, because the belief is that members' lives depend on how well the conversion process takes place.

Internal Dynamics: What Do Self-help Groups Do?

Self-help groups are the central components of national self-help organizations. Groups foster a collective solution to individual conditions, illnesses, and problems. The social technology aimed at solving the focal problem engages members at the group level. The term "self-help" is a bit of a misnomer since it actually denotes *mutual aid* and *reciprocity* among group members, in contrast to the servicing of the isolated self. Individuals assume responsibility for coping with their own problem(s), and at the same time, assist others, and are assisted themselves by others, in the process of negotiating the problems associated with their condition. Self-help is characterized by a reversal in the traditional relationship between expert helper and inexpert helpee (Riessman and Carroll 1995). The helper experiences increased self-esteem, social approval, and acceptance as a result of being a competent renderer of help. Self-help views personal experience as the basis for problem-solving such that the inexpert helpee becomes the help-giver as new members cycle through different stages of their experience with the group's focal issue. A new member of Monosomy 9p, for example, may have a child with the 9p genetic deficiency and little understanding of resources available to help the family cope with medical and educational situations that arise. A long-term member can talk about his or her experiences with medical professionals, schools, and surgery. Later, the new member shares his or her experience with an even newer member, thus fostering reciprocity.

Previous studies of self-help (Kurtz 1997) reveal six dimensions of group support and five dimensions of change relevant to how self-help groups do what they do. The first set is: "giving support, imparting information, conveying a sense of belonging, communicating experiential knowledge and teaching coping methods" (p.21). The second set includes: "identity transformation, empowerment, insight, reframing and formation of a new way of life" (p.24). Following Kurtz, I summarize these six dimensions.

Self-help participants understand giving support as "a combination of words and silent attention, personal disclosure and empathy [all of which encompass] the learning of coping strategies, having a sense of community, coping with public attitudes, getting factual information, attaining a spirit of hope, attaining self-confidence" (p.21). Giving support is a broad description of many self-help group processes that occur in face-to-face interaction. Imparting information establishes the state of knowledge concerning the group's focal issue and helps educate the public. In some cases it reduces stigma associated with illness. Affiliation is another dynamic with broad ramifications for group members. Participants in self-help gain a sense of belonging. Yet, this sense of belonging differs from affiliation with other types of organizations. Self-help is a "normative structure similar to a family, a religious organization" (p.22) and entails social networks and a loosely structured community devoted to common values in which "achieving a sense of belonging in the self-help community becomes a measure of successful identity change" (p.22).

Conversation is the key method of giving support, imparting information, and creating a sense of belonging. It is the mechanism by which health is restored. Communicating experiential knowledge in self-help occurs through discussion of personal stories. Participants discuss their personal struggles and triumphs in order to frame strategies for coping with illness and growing beyond the stigma it creates. Through ritualized storytelling, members create a conceptual framework for one another that enlightens and makes their personal troubles meaningful. The self-help literature offers innumerable examples of these narratives. Denzin's (1987) discussion of Alcoholics Anonymous is one of the best. Teaching coping skills is the last component of interpersonal interaction at the group level. Since learning is based on understanding the experience of others vis-à-vis one's own experiences, coping strategies are conveyed through discussion of examples drawn from everyday encounters and modeled in participants' behavior. The range of skills is considerable and depends on the unique experiences of group participants. Learning to cope in new ways occurs both within the context of formal meetings of groups and among individual members outside of formal meeting times.

Self-help members not only learn behavior-altering skills, but experience life changes as a result of practicing the skills acquired in the group. Identity transformation, empowerment, and personal insight are a few of the changes experienced by self-help participants. Positive identity transformation is a key goal for self-help group participants. The newcomer first identifies with group members on the basis of their similar experiences. As affiliation grows (Kurtz 1997:24–25):

> the recognition that she or he can achieve what the veteran member has attained moves the recruit to acquire the characteristics of the older member. Veteran members construct and model new ways of coping and being.

The process of identity transformation, whereby a spoiled, deviant, or stigmatized identity (Goffman 1963) is embraced as positive entails a conversion process (see e.g., Makela 1996, Denzin 1987, Rudy and Greil 1988). The process of conversion involves biographical reconstruction in which addicts become "recovered persons," and cancer patients become "cancer survivors" under this regime.[3] In order for reconstruction to take place, acceptance of the spoiled identity must take place. Acceptance of a spoiled identity may be in regards to one's own identity or another's stigmatized social role. Self-help groups of families of the mentally ill, for example, may have to accept the stigma attached to the label before the process of transforming that identity can take place. This acceptance is based on the principle that healing does not take place until the problem has been correctly diagnosed by the group member. In addition, identity transformation takes place in a group context so that further stigmatization is controlled. Discussion of the problem and its solution provides a "vocabulary through which members conceptualize and communicate about their illness" or that of a friend or family member (Kurtz 1997:25).

Becoming empowered—acting on one's behalf or on behalf of another person—is an important change that self-help members experience as a result of participation in the life of the self-help community. Since the group is composed of fellow sufferers, joint pursuit of goals and interests is likely to have an extraordinary effect on an individual's self-efficacy, and sense of personal control. An effective support system can neutralize or correct the sense of loss of bodily and mental function. Individuals suffering from physical problems accomplish this by fostering quality relationships with others who share the same condition. Through these quality relationships, having seen what others of equal standing can do for themselves and for one another, self-confidence grows and along with it the ability to commit to the process of recovery. Riessman and Carroll (1995:21) argue that people who:

> look to the smaller picture...achieve empowerment without relying on entrenched establishment authorities for help...In this sense, self-help represents not a rebellion against gigantism of the modern world but rather a return to the more governable limits of neighborhood, friends, family and self. In a world where problems are expanding, resources are thinning...and the voice of the individual is lost in the crowd, the friendly self-help group meeting around the corner seems just the place to take back one's lost sense of power, self-value and control.

Insight and reframing problems are also important components of self-help. Continued growth of self-esteem and self-efficacy depend on cognitive as well as behavioral development. In a study of family-oriented self-help, Kurtz (1997) observed how participants "learned to define the alarming and embarrassing behaviors of mental illness or alcoholism as symptoms of a disease rather than as intentional, immoral or foolish actions" (p.28). In doing so, an appraisal of immoral behavior was replaced by one that showed being responsible entailed seeking help. Membership and participation in self-help is an indicator of the desire to seek help and therefore assume responsibility for one's behavior.

Taking responsibility promotes well-being for several reasons. Affiliation improves performance due to shared experience, while gaining control over personality, cognition, and motivation leads to greater self-esteem (Katz 1993). For many self-help members, self-help represents a new community and a way of life. It represents a normative, narrative community in which participants join their individual story to that of others', and achieve empowerment and feelings of enhanced self-esteem. Transformation of identity involves becoming a member of the self-help community and participation takes place in an atmosphere of noncompetitiveness and cooperation. In this community, groups are self-sustaining rather than dependent on outside resources and create an egalitarian and tolerant network where norms of reciprocity operate.

The Origins of Self-Help: An Abbreviated History

In this section, I draw on Katz (1993) for a summary of the history of self-help. I also borrow from Hall's (1992) discussion of the rise of voluntary associations in the United States. Katz provides an overview of self-help as a type of cultural phenomenon spanning the modern era. He begins with friendly societies of the eighteenth and nineteenth centuries, which arose out of the premodern guilds and were precursors of today's self-help organizations. These self-governing, locally organized societies provided a kind of social insurance against ill fortune by donating food and money, subsidizing burials, and making loans available to their members, as well as arranging "club nights, outings, picnics, and holiday celebrations" (Katz 1993:5). The rise of associations such as these in the United States was "rooted in powerful social, political and economic forces which by the early eighteenth century had begun to erode the authority of family, church, and government throughout the colonies" (Hall 1992:17). Interestingly, compared to our current belief in the benefits of associational membership, there was considerable ambivalence about voluntary associations in premodern America since they were seen as consisting of "unfettered individuals pursuing their own interests" (p.20). Voluntary organizations were devoted to the study of the Bible and religion, and consisted of temperance groups, and tract societies. Benjamin Franklin's Junto Club, for instance, was a peer group devoted to self-improvement that discussed morals, politics, and natural philosophy in order to promote self-control and self-improvement in its members.

Mechanic societies in the early nineteenth century "were organized to politically, socially and economically empower craftsmen and small businessmen who had been, up to that point, virtual strangers to formal modes of organizational activity" (Hall 1992:141). During this time, trade unions and cooperatives were established to resolve problems associated with the Industrial Revolution. In the United States, large cohorts of immigrants came to rely on networks of former neighbors, family, and village to assimilate. Voluntary associations played a key role for these groups whose primary kinship identity was transformed into a national, albeit minority, identity in the United States (e.g., Irish-American, Italian-American, and so on).

Interestingly, temperance movements in the United States in the eighteenth and nineteenth centuries served as early examples of self-help that later blossomed into an effective anti-alcohol movement, promoting the experiment of Prohibition in the 1920s. The religiously oriented beliefs and organizational style of temperance were precursors of a reactivated movement in the 1930s and 1940s (White 1998) and later, prefigured the modern recovery movement (Wagner 1997).

In the postwar decades in the United States, self-help has come to signify locally organized groups with national affiliates aimed at providing material and emotional assistance to individuals experiencing some personal stigmatizing condition or problem. The most well-known self-help organization, Alcoholics Anonymous, was established in the 1930s. During the 1940s, groups dealing with families of children who were physically or emotionally ill or handicapped arose, followed by a number of special-purpose groups. By the 1950s, organizations dealing with juvenile mental retardation, cerebral palsy, hemophilia, and muscular dystrophy were well established. The International Conference on Social Work took place in 1954. It emphasized the theme of promoting social welfare through self-help and support groups. The Association for Retarded Children and the National Hemophilia Foundation are two examples of groups that publicized their focal problem in order to encourage professional and state support. Important recognition of self-help occurred in 1961 under the auspices of the Kennedy administration, wherein the Association for Retarded Children promoted the formation of a National Commission on Mental Illness and Mental Retardation. Further advances did not occur until the early 1970s. At that time, The National Institute of Mental Health, the Bureau of Health Education of the Centers for Disease Control, and the National Heart, Blood and Lung Institute held conferences on self-help. These conferences did not result in any specific state action but did legitimate self-help and self-care.

In 1970, the Hughes Act established the National Institute of Alcoholism and Alcohol Abuse, and in 1973, handicap reform was institutionalized by the Rehabilitation Act of 1973. The latter Act made it a crime to discriminate against the handicapped. By the late 1970s, self-help began to receive indirect support with the rise of third-party payments for treatment of various addictions whose members ended up in support groups after formal treatment. Third-party payments for alcoholism quadrupled from 1978–1984 (Peele 1989). During this time, conservative politicians disillusioned with the expansion of the welfare state called for decreasing public expenditures. The Omnibus Reconciliation Act of 1981 began the devolution of public policy with the reduction of federal spending for public programs and the consolidation of social welfare programs. It was argued that reduction in governmental involvement in health and human services would increase private entrepreneurial activities. Thus, during the period 1975 to 1985, self-help clearinghouses were established in New Jersey, California, New York, Illinois, and Minnesota. In 1989 and 1990, the National Institute of Mental Health established self-help research centers in Michigan and California. Oddly, despite devolution of state welfare policy, federal healthcare spending grew rather than declined during the 1980s and 1990s (Smith and Lipsky 1993).

The turning point in acceptance of self-help occurred in the 1980s (Hedrick, Isenberg, and Martini 1992). Recognition of self-help burgeoned in the form of media attention. Forums for discussion of self-help were as varied as Oprah Winfrey's talk show, the *Journal of the American Medical Association*, *People* magazine, and television docudramas. The latter often featured the disease of the week in the manner of characters afflicted with everything from AIDS to cancer. The state weighed in with the Surgeon General Everett Koop's Workshop on Self-Help and Public Health in 1987, providing strong institutional support for self-help. The Workshop led thirteen federal agencies to initiate projects aimed at stimulating self-help (Illinois Self-Help Coalition 1997). By the end of the twentieth century, as noted in Chapter One, the number of Americans using self-help was substantial. Estimates of participation range from between 6.5 and 15 million members, depending on the source of information. With this many Americans engaged in self-help, what processes led to the growth and permanence of the movement?

The Institutionalization of Self-Help

Social institutions are the structures that carry out essential social functions to maintain or improve community life in the economy, polity, and civil spheres. Institutions such as government, education, science, medicine, and families act as premier mechanisms for socializing individuals in these spheres of activity. In a very powerful sense, institutions structure social life because they are the rules of the game (North 1990) and they articulate with formal and informal organizations, associations, and groups. Institutions involve normative rules that enter into social life as facts and institutionalization is the process by which social behavior assumes a rule-like status in thought and action (DiMaggio and Powell 1983). Constitutional government, public education (and now home-schooling), free markets, and third-party payers in healthcare are all institutionalized in Western polities. Institutionalization involves the activities and mechanisms by which practices, structures, and behaviors such as these become taken for granted by actors ranging from individuals to corporations and societies. Institutionalized behavior is taken for granted because when justifications (i.e., legitimation) for action are needed, institutions carry their own rationales. Constitutional government, public education, and free markets, for instance, rely on individuals' beliefs in the sanctity of utilitarian self-interest in individualist polities. The processes by which a practice, symbol, network structure, or other social behavior becomes taken for granted are complex and one of the chief questions underlying social science investigation. Some researchers view organizations as the locus by which institutionalization occurs and others see institutionalization occurring at the societal or cultural level. Sometimes social movements are involved and other times the carriers of institutions are state actors and professions. In short, the central question is how marginalized actors and practices, particularly healthcare practices dominated by medical hegemony, become mainstream (Ruggie 2004).

Social movements become institutionalized by engaging the political system and then being coopted by it. Usually they pursue some form of noninstitutionalized political struggle, win some legal battles, and their reforms become laws and rights. Self-help did produce legal challenges but it was the diffusion of its form, the proliferation of its support groups by which it had its most profound impact on American culture. Formal diffusion was accompanied by support from important authorities in medicine, academia, and politics, and sustained by popular opinion.

Three different perspectives explaining the processes by which marginal social practices become rule-like are summarized by Schneiberg and Soule (2005). In the first perspective, institutionalization is a cultural enactment of some larger symbolic entity from which flows, in a top-down fashion, conceptual categories that explain contemporary societies (Jepperson 2002). These enactments reference broad cultural patterns in beliefs and behavior about how and why societies are ordered and organized the way they are. Individualism, the nation-state, economic rationality, and democracy are examples of conceptual categories that address the question of how and why societies are ordered and organized the way they are. Fire regulation

(Schneiberg 2002), education (Meyer 1977), the modern business organization (Meyer and Rowan 1977) and self-help are institutions consistent with explanations such as these. These conceptual categories are based on explanatory schemes that serve to legitimate all manner of beliefs and practices. In the process of institution-building in fire regulation, for instance, organizers might invoke "the language of efficiency and political order to justify" the development of for-profit organizations (Schneiberg and Soule 2005:127) or they might trade on the concepts of merit, equality, impartiality, and science to justify the creation of fire insurance associations. Similarly, self-help advocates often allude to the ideals of ascetic Protestantism (e.g., the importance of personal responsibility), which generates movement values associated with the practice of utilitarianism and self-reliance (e.g., returning the locus of control from doctors to individual patients).

In the second perspective, institutionalization results from diffusion of uncoordinated local practices. This process is the opposite of the top-down view of institutionalization as cultural expression. Local social practices become taken for granted in this framework in a three-step process. Innovation in a practice or behavior occurs as a random process, which is then adopted by individual actors at the local level as a solution to some problem. Other actors (e.g., movement organizers, business leaders) then imitate the innovators. The innovation slowly but steadily spreads among other actors and throughout the field. Legitimacy is acquired by all who imitate the practice, and actors take up the form or policy or practice regardless of whether it meets their actual needs. Using the fire insurance industry again, state actors seized on fire regulation through close monitoring of other states and imitated their rules even when they might have pursued other regulatory practices. Among self-help actors, diffusion occurs as independent organizational forms are created to meet healthcare needs that established medicine and social welfare services fail to provide. Later, groups adopt similar forms and practices to solve problems of unmet needs that might have been solved through other means. Alcoholics Anonymous (1935), Al-Anon (1951), Addicts Anonymous (1947) and Narcotics Anonymous (1953) were early founders whose twelve-step programs became the basis for all of the other anonymous groups such as Gamblers Anonymous (1957), Emotions Anonymous (1971), Co-dependents Anonymous (1986). The anonymous twelve-step organizational form became the template for organizations for which alternative practices could also have been successfully developed. The key mechanism in the diffusion model is that as the number of adopters increases, relevant authorities endorse their innovation, which gains legitimacy and becomes the norm. Physicians and other medical professionals who support the development of alternative practices such as self-help are crucial for institutionalization since they provide access to material and symbolic resources in mainstream medicine. This seems counterintuitive since alternative practices are likely to lead to fragmentation and disruption of medical hegemony over healthcare. So, why would they help in the diffusion of self-help, since self-help is a contested set of beliefs and practices? As the following chapters demonstrate, self-help organizers must finesse the acquisition of legitimacy from dominant interests themselves as a means for establishing their credibility. They do so by coopting professionals who act in the interests of self-help. Cooptation signals another route to institutionalization of self-help.

Political struggles over jurisdiction are a critical source of institution building. Usually these result from state-level crises (e.g., legislation, court rulings, creation of new agencies, etc.) which foster uncertainty and disrupt practices among local actors. Conflict between local actors ensues until compromise is reached, political reconstruction occurs, and institutionalization of new practices takes place. For self-help, this framework does not seem applicable because, Koop notwithstanding, the state had little impetus to directly shape the alternative sector, and little interest in the minor disputes between local actors over voluntary associations' jurisdiction. However, the state indirectly shaped the growth of self-help through its role as the largest purchaser of healthcare in the 1960s, which led to the fragmentation of medical professional hegemony (Scott et al. 2000), and opened the field to complementary and alternative practices. State deregulation of healthcare and the emergence of market logics in the 1980s led to even greater splintering of professional dominance and the burgeoning of self-help. Pressure from self-help advocates was considerable. Organizers were active at this time in framing alternative healthcare practices as superior to mainstream ones and highlighted the "disjuncture between medicine, which is oriented toward curing illness, and healthcare, which is oriented toward wellness and the prevention of illness" (Ruggie 2004:45–46). They offered self-help as an innovation by which prevention could be organized.

Not surprisingly, a fourth framework synthesizes the other three, explaining that the process of institutionalization is not just a cultural expression or local diffusion of organizational forms or a state-level political contest but all three. Although it is seductive to portray the emergence of self-help largely on the basis of universal themes like individualism (as some authors do below), or else as a consequence of unmet needs (as others do), the growth of self-help is a multilevel process that involves enactment of cultural scripts, diffusion, and socio-political conflict. As the premier challenger to institutionalized healthcare, self-help faces a number of problems in the process of enactment and diffusion that mainstream actors engaged in political contests do not. That is, how do challenger organizations acquire the necessary legitimacy from institutional sources when these sources represent their antagonists? In a very important sense, as much as self-help represents a legitimated, institutionalized set of beliefs and practices, it remains on the margins of institutionalized healthcare. The model just developed shows how enactment, diffusion, and politics foster the conditions under which self-help emerges and becomes taken for granted. These models help frame the basic demographic processes underlying the dramatic growth and stability of self-help.

Using Cultural Enactment, Organizational Diffusion, and the Politics of Self-Help to Map its Evolution

The self-help literature contains two main varieties of explanation of the origins and institutionalization of the self-help movement: ideo-logical (i.e., cultural enactment) and social-structural (i.e., organiza-tional diffusion). As I discussed above, ideological accounts emphasize the expression of universal themes in the practices, values, and beliefs of self-help. These explanations tend to focus on the cultural origins of particular groups and organizations. For example, Rice (1996) links the rise of Co-Dependents Anonymous with the widespread acceptance of psychotherapy, while Hurvitz (1976) claims that self-help (i.e., Alcoholics Anonymous) is a result of convergence of psy-chotherapeutic and religious traditions in American culture. Structural accounts emphasize the diffusion of practices as a result of changes in macrosocial phenomena, such as modernization, loss of traditional support systems, and decline of community. The central claim is that self-help arose to fill needs created by changes in tradi-tional support systems.

These two explanatory perspectives contain an underlying theme of self-help as a political actor facing the goliath of mainstream healthcare. While studies of self-help develop this theme in line with the frameworks of cultural enactment, diffusion, and politics, they do so rather obliquely. I therefore focus on the politics of self-help explicitly as a function of contests over legitimation. Legitimation of self-help involves cooptation of institutional actors who provide authoritative recognition of it. In Chapter Four I detail the processes involved and explore the evolution of patterns of legitimation for the entire population of self-help organizations in Chapter Five.

Cultural Enactment—Ideological Explanations

The "new age" Erhard Seminars Training movement (EST) of the 1970s is an extension of the psychology-based mental hygiene movement of the beginning of the twentieth century (Abraham 1988).[4] The mental hygiene movement (1910) arose in the moral vacuum of changing sociopolitical authority, which set the context for the process by which ascetic Protestant ideals became the basis for twentieth-century rationalization of organizational ideology and the eventual rise of self-help. Ascetic Protestantism generates social values such as utilitarianism, individualism, and self-control that are taken up by the mental hygiene and, later, self-help movements. The EST movement, like that of the earlier mental hygiene movement, is one vivid example of the persistence of hygienic utilitarianism today. It consists of two central ideas: 1) individual misfortune or suffering reflects the shortcoming of the individual, and consequently, 2) change is preeminently psychological or attitudinal. Psychological and attitudinal changes produce health and happiness that come about through elimination of troublesome beliefs, attitudes, and patterns of thinking. Like EST and the hygiene movement, self-help proposes to teach people skills to evaluate their own psyches. The solution offered is "the power to change some sort of stress with the environment into a purely internal stress and so to bring it under self-control" (Abraham 1988:760–761).

In another version of this cultural account (Rice 1996), increasing social fragmentation and repressive individual socialization produced a social movement organization modeled after the institutionalized twelve-step programs of Alcoholics Anonymous and Al-Anon, called Co-Dependents Anonymous (CoDA). CoDA represents the apex of the second-generation twelve-step programs. It is in the form of CoDA that the precepts of the therapeutic culture become adapted to "a transformation, still under way in the U.S. culture" which entails widespread acceptance of "liberation psychotherapy as a popular discourse" (Rice 1996:11). In this model, groups engage in identity reconstruction using universal themes of individualism and the Protestant ideal of the importance of self-control.

Similarly, Lasch (1984) discusses the impact of the therapeutic culture, although he does not address the issue of self-help directly. Psychoanalysis, Lasch argues, in the hands of Adler, Jung, and Rogers, became a "cult of personal health and fulfillment" armed with an implicit cultural critique (p.209). When this critique was combined with a nineteenth-century liberal Protestantism of the self-improvement variety, it produced a new technology of the self; a kind of spiritual eclecticism aimed at moral self-improvement.

The therapeutic culture in all these accounts provides the context within which contemporary self-help arises, especially given the self-interested ideals of the 1960s counterculture. Rienarman (1995) links the spread of self-help to *backlash* against the hedonistic 60s. He notes that "mass consumption and its indulgence ethic have created a culture in which growing numbers of people perceive an increasing number of ways to lose control" (p.101). The 1960s saw the use of drugs elevated to the level of political principle. The culture of pleasure and protest that characterized the 1960s is paralleled by a backlash in the form of a culture of temperance based on the Protestant ethic. With the decline of political protest movements of the 1960s there arose a collective response (in the form of the rise of psychotherapy and health consciousness) which focused on "individual responsibility—work, discipline, abstention, renunciation. Such practices were in harmony with the twelve-step movement" (p.103).[5]

Finally, Hurvitz (1976) describes self-help in terms of the conjunction of modern psychology and Lutheran confessional practices. His model straddles both the cultural enactment perspective and the diffusion perspective while linking broad cultural themes such as modern psychology to the origins of Peer Self-Help Psychotherapy Groups (PSHPGs), such as Alcoholics Anonymous, Recovery Inc., Synanon, and others. The central argument is that PSHPGs were formed as a sort of populist response to the demands of an "increasing number of Americans who needed inexpensive and effective psychiatric and psychological" care during the Great Depression (p.283). Self-help developed from religious and secular world-views that converged in American life. Like most writers on the subject, Hurvitz links the American preference for psychological explanations with broad cultural institutions under the auspices of individualism, self-reliance, mutual aid, humanitarianism, and nondenominationalism. The religious tradition of small-group activity characterized by confession, repentance, restitution, and mutual help paralleled the tradition of democracy, humanitarianism, individualism, and a psychological view of human behavior. The result was an organizational form, not just an ideology, in which conversation became the primary mechanism for healing and mutual aid fused with an ideology of individualism and self-reliance.

These instances of cultural enactment show how various societal-level symbolic categories diffuse over time and become part of self-help organizations and practices. The process is a top-down one in which taken-for-granted practices and forms get encoded in new organizational forms such as group psychotherapy and self-help. In the next set of explanations, the origins and ultimate institutionalization of self-help is not a function of cultural elements but of problematic structural ones. These generate local problem-solving efforts by social movement organizations that spread across the population.

Organizational Diffusion—Social-Structural Explanations

Social-structural explanations of the origins of self-help tend to be breakdown explanations. These models depict societal tendencies in which self-help groups are seen as individual local problem-solving responses to the breakdown of traditional informal support systems centered on a strong family and meaningful community relationships. For example, Makela's (1996) study of Alcoholics Anonymous is based on the underlying assumption that AA groups are a response to the changes in traditional informal support systems that give rise to a particular manifestation of community in the form of the AA group. Riessman and Carroll (1995:17) detail the core ideas of this perspective:

> Many communal supports that once gave our forebears a sense of group solidarity have disappeared from modern life, leaving us without an anchor or sense of tribe. In their place are substituted the cold comforts of competition, rampant individualism, bureaucracy, the TV set, and the prying eye of the technostate.

People form self-help groups as a response to environmental destruction, inefficient medical care, loss of a sense of belonging or shared beliefs, substance abuse, crime, stratification, poverty, breakdown of the family, and increased mobility. Borman (1992) expresses this bluntly: families no longer have "the resources to provide adequate assistance. Added to family instability and the increasing number of single-parent households is an increasingly high mobility rate. It is easy to see why self-help groups have become quasi-extended families" (pp. xxii–xxiii).

A related social-structural theme is that self-help relieves some of the financial burden placed on mainstream health and human services administration. Current health and human services cannot adequately provide for the needs of millions of people requiring services. Therefore, in a world of expanding medical needs and shrinking medical resources, self-help groups fill a niche in service provision. As this form of organizing gains prominence, its use spreads and others borrow its practices to meet their own needs.

The Politics of Self-Help

The demystification of medical knowledge over the course of 60 years has led to increased distrust and cynicism in traditional medicine: alternative modalities such as Chinese medicine and homeopathy have become more popular and legitimate in the eyes of potential consumers. Riessman and Carroll (1995) note that erosion of trust in medical science led to reforms during the 1960s, which produced ideas such as patient "empowerment, prevention, self-help and self care, patients' rights, consumer advocacy... increased sharing of information between doctors and patients and the awarding of patients a more active voice in their own treatment" (p.92). Consequently, the rise of patient rights and advocacy contributed greatly to the acceptance of self-help.

As a movement that challenges the institutional authority of mainstream medicine, self-help engages in sociopolitical conflict, although some of its organizations do so more directly than others. Still, our understanding of self-help might be broadened considerably if we were to examine how self-help functions as a challenger movement. To do so would entail looking at openings in the political system and the manner in which self-help organizers take advantage of these. One theoretical model proposes that institutionalization takes place as a result of conflict between actors who struggle, compromise, and institute new practices and forms. There are a number of ways of understanding how this occurs. Political opportunity theories (Meyer 2004; Meyer and Minkoff 2004) would suggest that self-help emergence and institutionalization followed dramatic changes over a forty- to fifty-year period that marked the transformation of healthcare governance systems (Scott et al. 2000). Changes took place as the professional dominance of physicians gave way to federal involvement and increasing fragmentation of the healthcare field. Soon, industry deregulation shifted authority away from both physicians and the state as health-care came to reflect market reforms. In addition, a burgeoning health rights social movement in the 1970s signaled weakness of the authorities to challenges from outside the system (Starr 1982). Self-help blossomed as a consequence of changes in professional governance regimes and state expansion into healthcare and increased social movement activity. Katz (1992a, 1992b) for example, argues that increasing medical professional hegemony and declining state support for social services shaped self-help, which then arose to fill unmet health and human service needs. Professional dominance entails rising costs, impersonal medical bureaucracies, and loss of control and dignity. In the face of physician resistance and state indifference, organizers built organizations that were cost effective, personalistic, and returned control and dignity to the consumer-patient. Their cultural template for organizing was something quite simple and taken for granted: the nineteenth-century temperance meeting, itself based on the religious revival. In these meetings, public confession, the sharing of personal stories of fall from grace and redemption, provided the catalyst for participation and membership, and structured what became known as the local self-help group (White 1998).

Organizational Ecology and the Self-Help Movement

These different explanations of self-help emergence and institutionalization help us understand the fundamental social and cultural contexts within which self-help grew. However, because of a lack of comprehensive data, none ever actually examined the patterns of organizational formation and dissolution, legitimation and competition, and resource use that were vital to self-help. That is, lacking self-help demographic data, no research addresses the basic issue of how self-help organizational forms are reproduced and evolve over time, nor offers a very comprehensive description of the processes by which the self-help organizational form becomes institutionalized. Rather, each framework emphasizes one aspect of the process. The ideological explanation provides the cultural context, the social-structural explanation emphasizes diffusion of practices based on unmet needs, and the political one helps us understand the role that political struggles take in shaping the evolution of self-help. But because there is no systematic link between the movement and its organizations in any of these explanations, the way in which ideology, diffusion, and politics combine to foster the self-help movement, its trajectory and ultimate persistence remains an empirical mystery. For example, are some authorities more important for the emergence or for the dissolution of self-help organizations, and how?

An organizational ecology is useful for the task of answering questions such as these and explaining the institutionalization of self-help because it provides the foundation for empirical analysis of these explanations based on the self-help movement as a system of organizations. Combined with the notion of diffusion, culture, and political contention, this approach describes the evolution of self-help and several of the mechanisms expected to drive that evolution: legitimation and competition. Legitimation shifts the distribution of power across and between organizational fields while competition alerts us to the differential allocation of material resources that influences the dynamics of organizations in the population. This framework provides an important theoretical tool for the task of explaining the spread of self-help because it describes the effects of organizational and institutional forces. Both legitimation and competition are vital for self-help founding and dissolution, a dynamic that highlights the processes by which these organizations create an independent ecological niche in the alternative health and human services sector (Maton 1989). In the next chapter I depict these dynamics by exploring the growth and diversification of these organizations as they capture different health-care markets. The framework I begin with is the diffusion one in which instances of the form emerge and spread across time and space. To the extent that these organizations capture different markets for their services, legitimation of the form diffuses as well. This is not simply a speculative observation. The chapter following the next one begins our examination of how legitimation of the form diffuses. While the empirical emphasis is on diffusion, political contention driven by social movement actors who borrow from a wealth of symbolic cultural elements forms the background for the study of the evolution of self-help.

3

From Small Beginnings: Growth and Diversification

Although a considerable amount of research on modern self-help has been undertaken during the last three decades, studies have tended to concentrate on individual groups and tertiary movements such as the cancer survivors movement or the recovery movement, their function, and constituents.[1] In fact, an emphasis in self-help research on the study of tertiary movements has led to the neglect of the larger phenomenon of self-help itself, which includes cancer survivors and recovering addicts as well as children with autism, and others. Having explored in the previous chapter what self-help organizations are, what they do, and how they become taken for granted, this chapter will address the question of the dynamics of self-help as a whole: How did self-help grow, and what organizational dynamics account for changes in its growth, its decline, and ultimate persistence? The framework I begin with is the diffusion one—instances of a form emerge and spread across time and space as they are adopted by organizers. This lays the foundation for later explorations of how legitimation (public recognition) and competition for material resources influence the evolution of self-help. To the extent that these organizations capture different markets for their services, legitimation of the form spreads.

This chapter describes the dynamics of growth, decline, and the ultimate persistence of the self-help population; its formal diversification, and the extent to which its subpopulations gain market share. Theoretically, I am focusing on the diffusion of practices that aggregate at the national organizational population level to explain the institutionalization of self-help. Empirically, I explicitly use an organizational-ecological framework to map the trajectory of these patterns to show how expansion of self-help is remarkably similar to the trajectories of commercial, bureaucratic, and social movement populations. Establishing comparability among a variety of different organizational forms reveals that the organizational ecology framework is versatile and can be extended to understand a broad range of very different types of organizations and movements.

In order to investigate the dynamics of the formation of self-help, the first section of the chapter discusses case selection for creation of a self-help database and provides a brief theoretical background using organizational ecology. Explanations of the rise of self-help, discussed in the last chapter, can be built upon by research that empirically addresses the growth and decline of self-help groups. It is particularly important to conduct a systematic survey of the growth, decline, and persistence of self-help organizations because it shows how noncommercial (voluntary) organizational populations vie for resources and how resource partitioning takes place among them. Past research has examined population diversification, concentration, and partitioning in a number of commercial sectors such as the U.S. recording and film industries (Dowd 2004; Mezias and Mezias 2000), microbreweries (Carroll and Swaminathan 2000), restaurants (Hannan and Freeman 1989), and among social movements (Haider-Markel 1997; see Baum 1996 and Carroll and Hannan 2000, pp. 269–270 for review). Resource partitioning, which describes why some organizational fields are dominated by a few organizations and how other organizations survive under those conditions (see Carroll and Swaminathan 2000), lends itself to predictions about the expected relationships between various classes of self-help organizations. An important question this chapter addresses is: Do the same conditions that generate resource partitioning in commercial sectors promote the phenomenon in the alternative health and human services sector, at least with respect to this population of organizations?

The second section of the chapter describes the actual patterns of organizational growth, decline, and persistence in the self-help population. Case studies and historical descriptions of the development of self-help argue that the population experienced "phenomenal growth" during the latter half of the twentieth century. Katz (1993) and others (e.g., Powell 1987; Riessman 1985) identify the 1960s as a period of considerable expansion of self-help. I test these observations and examine founding and disbanding rates, and formal diversification over a forty-five-year period. Subpopulations emerged during this time and gained access to resources in specialty niches that had not been previously developed, such as gastroenterology, abuse and violence, and genetics. Knowing changes in the distribution of organizations in the population in these functional areas provides the basis for generating insights into how social processes, such as specialization and resource partitioning, work. For example, it has been shown that founding rates decline because crowding in organizational populations limits access to resources for new organizations (e.g., see Carroll and Hannan 2000). However, in mature populations, a few large organizations eventually come to dominate a sector or market, and new organizations spring up to take advantage of specialty niches that remain open (Carroll 1985). It is theoretically interesting to wonder if this theory, which has been examined for commercial organizations, also predicts similar developments among self-help. That is, does the emergence of large dominant *subpopulations* of self-help organizations limit access to resources by other organizations? With regard to noncommercial populations, Tucker et al. (1988) suggest that this might be so.

The third section of this chapter examines these expectations. I analyze resource partitioning in the self-help population by determining market share of specialists and generalists (defined below) in eighteen self-help subpopulations (Powell 1987). I examine the extent to which concentration occurs within the two main types of self-help: social welfare and medical. Instead of focusing on the dominance of individual self-help organizations, I extend resource partitioning theory by trying to understand how the theory works with dominant firms in several *subpopulations* of organizations. In effect, I explore cross-population effects. Specifically, I examine trends in specialization among subpopulations, and resource concentration among both generalist and specialist organizations (and not just generalists alone as the theory suggests).

What we learn from this chapter is that 1) the growth, decline, and persistence of self-help resembles the dynamics and diversification of a variety of commercial and noncommercial organizational populations; 2) the relationship between diversification, resource use, and concentration is an unusually complex one. While the self-help market overall is dominated by specialists (in contrast to expectations of resource partitioning), the main historical trend is away from increasing specialization and generalist concentration, and toward greater generalism among organizations (again, in direct contrast to expectations). There is a strong tendency toward *less* concentration in both social welfare and medical subpopulations, as well as less concentration within specialist populations and (surprisingly) generalist populations. I discuss the implications of these results in the final section.

Creating a Self-Help Database

One of the most challenging aspects of this book was construction of an original database of life histories of all active national self-help organizations in the United States between 1955 and 2000. Since there has been no comprehensive research on the demography of the self-help organizational population, data therefore had to be compiled first.

Case Selection

In the late 1990s I created an original database of life histories of all active national self-help organizations in the United States between 1955 and 2000.[2] I chose to focus on national self-help organizations for several reasons. National self-help organizations promote better-developed support programs among local chapters, meetings and groups; provide stability and predictability; and, have a more diverse membership and a stronger leadership structure than unaffiliated groups (Borkman 1999; Powell 1987, 1990). Stability and predictability influence longevity, a key feature in the growth and diversification of the population and an issue of central interest in analyzing the dynamics of this population. Lastly, self-help organizations almost always attempt to establish a national presence in order to reach as many potential members as possible who share their condition, problem or illness, and as such, are usually engaged in formalizing their programs and structures.

While this operationalization has it limitations, it also has clear advantages. Naturally, it would be optimal to construct a comprehensive database using all self-help groups, chapters, meetings, organizations, networks, and their members from the early twentieth century through the present time. However, to have organized the kind of prospective study this calls for would have taken the kind of foresight neither researchers nor practitioners had. Instead, examining retrospective data on established self-help organizations using the best available resources provides an important opening into the dynamics of these unique kinds of organizations and the movement itself.

The Encyclopedia of Associations editions 1 through 36 (Gale Research) serves as the primary source of data and case selection for this project. Case selection is supplemented by *The Self-Help Sourcebook* editions 1–7 (White and Madara 2002) and *IRS Exempt Organization*

Microrecord Files. The database itself was constructed from a variety of sources that include *The Encyclopedia of Associations* (Gale Research Co.), covering the years 1955–2000; *Index Medicus-Medline, Congressional Information Service, Sociological and Psychological Abstracts, the New York Times Index, the U.S. Department of Commerce—Bureau of Economic Analysis, and the U.S. Department of Labor-Office of Education, National Center for Education Statistics.* Measures based on these additional sources are discussed in Chapters Five and Six (see also Archibald 2004).

The *Encyclopedia of Associations* contains historical information on all self-declared national membership organizations, including voluntary associations devoted to providing health and human services. Each edition and organizational entry of the *Encyclopedia of Associations* consists of a detailed year-by-year record that includes, but is not limited to, organizational founding date, organizational status (e.g., disbanding and changes in name), organizational services, social technology, and membership for all national self-help organizations. Only self-help organizations that identified themselves as "self-help" or those providing peer-to-peer support groups were selected. These were largely consistent with White and Madara's listings (2002). Unfortunately, self-identified self-help organizations may have become overrun by professionals without noting this change in the organizations' status.[3]

Many of the strengths of the *Encyclopedia of Associations* are discussed in Minkoff (1995). Martin, Baumgartner, and McCarthy (2005) show that coverage provided by the *Encyclopedia* is comprehensive. Despite its comprehensive coverage, some national self-help organizations may not appear in the *Encyclopedia of Associations* because they are too short-lived (i.e., those failing within a year). This criterion limits variation in organizational life spans to at least a year. It is a reflection of the nature of building a national organization rather than a specific bias on the part of the *Encyclopedia.*

Measuring Growth, Decline, and Diversification

Founding, Disbanding, and Density

The founding rate is defined as the rate of entry of new organizations into the self-help population during each observation period over the course of the history of the population. Organizations may be created *de novo*, they may have been acquired by other organizations, or they may have been reorganized and restructured. Organizational disbanding or failure is defined as exit of an organization from the self-help population. Organizations are defined as either active or defunct. Of the 589 self-help organizations active over the course of the forty-five-year period, 110 disbanded (18.7 percent). Lastly, population density is the total number of active organizations in the population during each observation period (Hannan and Freeman 1989). This measure is the cumulative total of active organizations at time t, net disbandings. Fig. 3.1 shows the irregular patterns of founding and disbanding over time. I discuss these patterns in Detailing Trends (below).

Diversification

The resource niche for an organization is its place among other organizations and consists of all the resources that sustain the population of organizations in it, including constraints that limit it (Hannan and Freeman 1989). Self-help consists of organizations using resources in two primary niches: social welfare and medicine. These niches consist of a number of organizational populations with social technologies oriented toward addressing a full range of conditions, illnesses, and stigma from spina bifida to stuttering.[4] To understand diversification, I divide these two main niches into eighteen self-help subpopulations, defined by Powell (1987) as:

Social Welfare:
- relationship (e.g., marriage, divorce, adoption, widowhood)
- status (e.g., sexuality, women, race/ethnicity, gender dysphoria)
- alcohol, drug addiction
- other addictions (e.g., food, sex, gambling, codependency)
- reproduction, children (e.g., high-risk pregnancy)
- abuse, violence (e.g., incest, self-mutilation, destructive relationships)
- grief (e.g., loss, death)
- mental illness (e.g., obsession-compulsion, depression)
- physical disability, autism, retardation
- legal (e.g., prostitution, family of prisoners)

Medical:
- cancer
- neurology (e.g., pain, sleep, stroke, paraplegia, head injury, fatigue)
- gastroenterology
- eye, ears, nose, and throat

- disease, infections, autoimmune disease, diabetes
- hormones, genetics, metabolic growth and development
- skin, burns, facial reconstruction
- respiratory, circulatory, and pulmonary illnesses

Specialists and Generalists

I define specialist and generalist organizations in terms of the extent and pattern of their resource use. Some organizations depend on financial resources to survive. For voluntary associations, such as self-help, the main resource is human capital, typically arising from organizational membership.[5] Since self-help groups are controlled by constituents whose problem or illness the group has been constructed to address, those conditions that require professional involvement raise special issues for self-help members. Self-help can involve expert professionals: an ambiguous relationship that the literature on self-help is at great pains to detail (see Kurtz 1999). Some types of self-help limit involvement to only those experiencing the focal condition. Others encourage a range of participants such as caregivers, families, and even professionals. For self-help organizations dealing with medical trauma, genetic dysfunction, cancer, and other life-threatening conditions, participation by medical professionals is essential to securing information, access to resources, and advancing knowledge of the treatment of traumatic conditions.

Some researchers label true self-help as only member-run organizations (Katz 1993; Kurtz 1999) although this is disputed by others who argue that professional involvement may form a continuum, with certain groups prohibiting professionals (e.g., the twelve-step organizations) and other groups welcoming them (Shepherd et al. 1999). One way to conceptualize the continuum is in terms of specialists and generalists. Most people tend to think of self-help organizations as specialists insofar as their technologies and issue areas are directed at specific constituencies, usually beneficiaries, for whom a particular condition, problem, or illness is salient. Alcoholics end up in addiction niches and those with skin conditions go to groups organized by the Sjogren's Syndrome Foundation. Individuals in each niche constitute a market, as it were. However, since some self-help organizations include family and friends as well as professionals, their product market is more inclusive and the interests of the groups must expand to incorporate these additional members. Doing so alters how the organization fulfills its mission. These organizations are self-help generalist organizations.

Self-help organizations that limit membership to those with the focal problem (e.g., alcoholism, stuttering, lung cancer, widowhood) are defined in this study as specialist organizations while those extending membership more broadly to include family members and even professionals are generalists.[6] The central point is that growth and diversification in the population follow from how self-help organizations differentiate themselves along the specialist-generalist continuum not only in terms of their core issue areas but importantly in inclusiveness their membership.

Concentration of Resources

Concentrated industries are those with resource monopolies. Industries that experience the greatest concentration have a few large enterprises (typically generalists) who, over the history of the population, gain the greatest share of the market (Boone, Carroll, and Witteloostuijn 2002). Voluntary associations gain market share of human capital. In the following analyses, I focus on market share of membership and the extent to which a few organizations monopolize self-help constituencies. Carroll, Dobrev, and Swaminathan (2003) use a concentration measure based on the top four largest firms. Following this study, concentration here refers to the proportion of the market that is controlled by the four largest self-help organizations based on the size of the constituency.

Applying Organizational Ecology to Self-Help: How Diversification, and Resource Partitioning Contribute to Population Expansion

Organizational ecologists are interested in why there are so many different organizational forms (Hannan and Freeman 1977). Banks, schools, medical practices, and human service agencies are examples of organizational forms. Organizational forms are classes of organizations defined by bounded sets of common organizational features such as their structures, practices, members, and routines (Hannan and Freeman 1989). In this theoretical perspective, new organizational forms emerge and old ones die out because of the operation of selection and adaptation. Selection occurs when social forces in the organizational environment promote organizational forms based on the optimal combination of stable organizational characteristics. Adaptation is the process whereby organizations adjust their routines and structures to fit often turbulent environmental conditions. Environmental conditions may be changes in regulatory statutes or shifts in markets. For example, deregulation of banking generated the phenomenon whereby organizations that were not previously known as providing financial services became competitors with those who did (Carroll and Hannan 2000). Successful selection and adaptation results in greater longevity. Selection processes explain the rise and decline of self-help because the formation and subsequent disbanding of self-help organizations is based on an organizational structure which, like most voluntary organizations, has little built-in flexibility for adapting to changing environmental conditions once it is established (Twombly 2003). Changes in the structure of the *population* occur because association members come and go, and create other organized groups to fill a variety of niches. Self-help organizations do not adapt their structures, practices, and programs to changing environmental conditions as much as their members disband them and create new organizations.

Organizational forms are embedded in network relationships facilitating resource flows (Carroll and Hannan 2000). Commonalities consist of core and peripheral features, usually goals, authority relations, technologies, and strategies that are encoded in organizational structures and routines (Scott 2003). Organizational forms resonate at a cultural level (i.e., people recognize what a bank, school, medical practice, or human service agency is). The form is therefore a kind of identity (Carroll and Hannan 2000). Organizations that are bound by a similar identity constitute a population of organizations and experience similar problems with respect to maintaining access to resources. Organizational ecologists analyze the niches of these resources because a central research question focuses on competition among organizations and how this influences the emergence of new organizations and the failure of others. Competition among organizations depends on the extent to which market niches overlap and resources are partitioned. Resource overlap increases competition along these dimensions while specializing—resource partitioning—decreases competition (Carroll and Swaminathan 2000).

Resource partitioning reflects the extent to which organizations attempt to manage competition for resources in order to thrive. The theory typically is used to explain the emergence of specialist organizations in industries characterized by a high degree of concentration or dominance by a few large organizations. Organizations do so by targeting services, products, and supplies to various market segments (Carroll and Hannan 2000). Some target to homogeneous segments and others to narrow segments. Types of strategies are not mutually exclusive, such that the former (generalists) and the latter (specialists) may partition a niche and share its resources. Carroll and Swaminathan (2000) show how specialist organizations, in the brewing industry, take advantage of concentrated (i.e., monopolized) markets to fashion a niche that protects them from competition with other breweries. Similarly, Haider-Markel (1997) demonstrates that interest groups avoid direct competition by adapting to different issue niches (i.e., specializing), and Ruef, Mendel, and Scott (1998) detail the ameliorative effects of resource partitioning on competition in the healthcare sector. For both commercial and noncommercial organizations, control of resource niches is important (see Baum 1996). Market concentration in industries is likely to increase the generalist failure rate because a few large organizations end up using all of a sector's resources. Concentration will lower the founding rate of other generalist organizations, again, because a few large generalist organizations dominate resource use, which inhibits the entry of new ones. There is only one Alcoholic Anonymous, for instance, just as there is only one Microsoft. However, the paradox of generalist concentration is that through the partitioning of resources, specialist organizations thrive because they do not directly compete with generalists. That is, over time, while there may be only one AA or Microsoft, there are many addiction groups and many software companies.

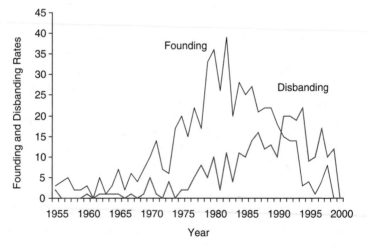

Figure 3.1   Founding and Disbanding Rates of Self-Help Organizations, 1955–2000

Under resource partitioning, the founding rate of specialists tends to be high and the failure rate is low as the population ages (Baum 1996; Carroll and Hannan 2000).

Detailing Trends: the Shape of the Movement

Self-Help Growth, Decline, and Persistence

Founding Rates

Fig. 3.1 presents founding and disbanding rates for the population of self-help organizations in this study. During the early period of the population, from the 1950s throughout the 1960s, the founding rate remained fairly steady. Until 1969, the average number of self-help foundings was about 3.5 per year. After 1969, the population experienced unprecedented growth in founding rates. Until this time the founding rate remained below ten organizations founded per year. Then in 1971, nearly fifteen self-help organizations form. A year later, there is a large drop in the founding rate that not only recovers but exceeds the highest previous rate. This pattern of large jumps followed by a year at a lower rate occurs throughout the middle period. In 1982, the founding rate peaked at thirty-nine organizations. Organizations founded that year include a wide array of subpopulations such as Children of Alcoholic Parents (alcohol), Chronic Granulomatosis Disease Association (genetic disorder), and Datcable/HI (disabled).

After 1982, the founding rate begins an equally precipitous decline until the end of the century. The year following 1982 witnessed only twenty organizational foundings. This number rose to twenty-eight the next year before slowly dropping off. The greatest decline occurred between 1993 and 1994 when the self-help founding rate dropped from fourteen per year to three per year. In the meantime, the rate at which self-help organizations disbanded shows a slow but steady increase over the observation period. While the self-help literature provides accounts of specific organizational foundings, there is little discussion of their dynamics. This figure shows how the population itself changed.

Organizational Disbanding Rates

During population emergence, from the 1950s throughout the 1970s, the disbanding rate remained steadily low. Until 1976, the average number of self-help disbandings was under 1.5 per year. This translates into about half as many disbandings as foundings. After 1976, the population began to experience much higher disbanding rates. These elevated dissolution rates peaked in the early 1990s at around twenty organizations a year. The rate of disbanding during the 1990s is higher than founding. However, because of the accumulated mass of organizations founded prior to the 1990s, the overall rate of decline in the self-help population is slow. The overall rate of change in this population is depicted by the shape of the density curve in fig. 3.2.

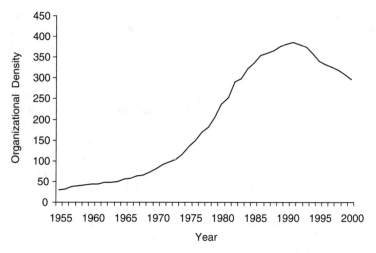

Figure 3.2   Organizational Density, Self-Help Organizations, 1955–2000

Density
The graph in fig. 3.2 depicts the density function for self-help organizations over the forty-five-year period. The density of organizations in the population at each time period is a cumulative function of the number of organizations at each period, taking into account the difference between foundings and disbandings. While the self-help literature provides historical accounts regarding the general formation of the population, there is little research on population dynamics. Persistence of self-help organizations therefore remains unknown.

The shape of the density curve in the second graph in fig. 3.2 is an inverted U-shape. The figure shows a long left-hand tail from the origins of the population through the mid-1970s. There is sustained but slow growth during the first twenty years of development of the population

(1955–1975). Consistent with the significant rise in founding rates, the population of self-help organizations experiences more accelerated growth in the late 1970s and early 1980s. Inspection of the first two graphs shows that the pattern of continual, then accelerated growth in self-help is due to a considerable increase in the ratio of foundings to disbandings around the 1970s. The steady acceleration of the density curve bears this out.

The founding rate, however, peaks in 1982 and begins to decline, while the rate of disbanding accelerates starting in the late 1970s. This pattern of declining founding rates and heightened disbandings causes the density curve to slow, finally peaking in 1991. During that year, 382 self-help organizations were active in the population. This is the largest number of self-help organizations active at one time during the forty-five-year observation period. From the early 1990s through the end of the century, the number of active self-help organizations begins to decline at about the same rate that it grew. Technically, the number of organizational disbandings outnumbers foundings during the last decade of the twentieth century. The reversal of births to deaths of self-help organizations reflects the positioning (or concentration/dominance) of larger, more durable organizations in the population: a common pattern in long-lived organizational populations (Barron 1999). I examine this possibility in the final section.

Overall, the shape of these distributions is remarkably similar to those found in commercial and bureaucratic as well as other social movement and nonprofit organizational populations. A comparison of the structure of this population to other empirical distributions (e.g., fig. 7.3 Carroll and Hannan 2000:156; fig. 2 in Minkoff 1994:954) demonstrates the reliability of the ecological framework for diverse populations.

Self-Help Diversification

Self-help founders represent the earliest groups. Founders in the self-help population cover a range of specialties from addiction organizations to those addressing heart disease and mental illness. Diversification is important in understanding how self-help organizations fill a variety of functional niches in the population. Prior studies of self-help organizations have been limited to historical accounts of the growth of self-help or case studies focusing on single organizations, therefore no systematic research on the distribution of these components of the alternative health and human service sector exists, although the information is readily available. To get a better understanding of how different self-help subpopulations emerge, I discuss the earliest founders and then investigate the distribution of specialty niches in detail as it unfolds after 1955.

The first expectation is that there will be a few founding organizations represented by alcohol/drug addiction groups, and groups dealing with families of children who were physically or emotionally ill or handicapped during the earliest periods of the history of self-help. These organizations emerged to fill particular gaps in health and human services (Katz 1993). In later periods, the population is expected to diversify to include organizations addressing a wide range of problems and conditions because of continuing gaps in services and because it will be easier to use a form that is already legitimated and increasingly available (Carroll and Hannan 2000).

Based on preliminary examination of individual founding organizations, the first few self-help founders are indeed alcohol/drug addiction groups. Parents of handicapped children are also represented, but not as prominently as expected. Founders include Alcoholics Anonymous (1935), Al-Anon (1951), Addicts Anonymous (1947), and Narcotics Anonymous (1953). Other early self-help organizations include medical groups devoted to blindness (Associated Blind 1938), mental retardation (National Association for Retarded Children 1953; Center for Family Support 1953), heart disease (Mended Hearts Club 1951), and psychological groups focusing on mental health (Recovery, Inc. 1937; The Bridge 1954). Self-help founders also consist of social service organizations dealing with homosexuality (Daughters of Bilitis 1955), divorce (Divorce Anonymous 1949; Judean Society 1952), and prisoners (Friends Outside 1955). The self-help population is fairly diverse to begin with and includes a range of medical organizations (from asthma to mastectomies) as well as social welfare organizations (from sexual identity to adoption).

Self-help organizations identify their functional niche, for data collection purposes in the *Encyclopedia*, based on the categories described in the Measures Section. I use Powell (1987), and Katz (1993) classificatory schemes for combining these functional areas. Some of the functional areas have been collapsed (e.g., in the medical category, respiratory, circulatory, and pulmonary groups were combined into a single category) because there were only one or two organizations devoted to a particular specialty. Self-help organizations are ostensibly functional specialists, and much of their activity regarding founding and disbanding is linked to securing the resources

Table 3.1 Percent Yearly Active National Self-Help Organizations in Each Subpopulation, 1955–2000

Organizational Subpopulations	1955	1965	1975	1985	1995	2000
Social Welfare						
Relationship	23.3	28.0	20.7	15.2	12.3	11.8
Alcohol, Drug Addiction	16.7	12.0	7.8	6.2	6.4	6.4
Mental Illness	13.3	12.0	7.8	5.0	5.8	5.7
Status	3.3	4.0	10.3	11.1	9.7	9.1
Other Addictions	3.3	8.0	4.3	4.0	3.3	3.4
Reproduction, Children	3.3	2.0	2.6	5.3	4.7	5.5
Physical Disability, Autism, Retardation	3.3	6.0	5.2	6.2	4.7	4.1
Legal	3.3	4.0	1.7	2.8	3.1	3.0
Abuse, Violence	0.0	2.0	3.4	4.6	3.3	3.7
Grief	0.0	0.0	5.2	6.8	6.4	6.4
Medical						
Eye, Ears, Nose Throat	13.3	10.0	9.5	6.8	5.6	6.4
Neurology, Paraplegia	6.7	6.0	8.6	8.7	9.7	9.8
Respiratory, Circulatory, Pulmonary	6.7	2.0	1.7	1.5	2.2	1.4
Cancer	3.3	2.0	2.6	2.5	1.4	1.4
Gastroenterology	0.0	2.0	1.7	2.2	3.6	3.0
Disease, Infections	0.0	2.0	3.4	3.1	4.5	4.7
Genetics, Metabolic Growth	0.0	0.0	0.9	4.3	8.6	9.8
Skin, Burns, Reconstructive Surgery	0.0	0.0	2.6	3.7	4.5	4.4
Number of Organizations (100%)	30	50	116	323	359	296

offered by a particular organizational niche (Baum and Oliver 1996). Generalist self-help organizations exist insofar as the target of their resource use involves constituencies other than members with the focal condition. We might call them general-specialists in comparison to other organizational forms, but since the comparison lies within self-help, I simply label them generalists.

Table 3.1 shows the distribution of self-help organizations by functional categories over the forty-five-year observation period. The percentages represent the number of active organizations in each category during the selected year. I have sorted the data by prevalence in 1955 and present data for each decade only (rather than year to year) to get a sense of the general patterns in niche specialization.

In the early years of the population's history, the majority of groups occupied two niches among the eighteen different subpopulations: in relationship support (23.3 percent) and alcohol and drug addictions (16.7 percent). Relationship organizations include those encompassing the recently widowed or divorced, as well as twelve-step groups serving as support for friends, relatives, family, spouses, and partners of alcoholics, substance abusers, gamblers, and other addicts. Addicts themselves constituted the second most prevalent functional area. Groups addressing functional areas that include mental illness (e.g., Schizophrenics Anonymous, Autism Network International), and those devoted to eye/ear/nose/throat (e.g., National Retinitis Pigmentosa Foundation) were the third most prevalent functional area, along with groups focusing on problems associated with neurology and paraplegia.

Ten years later the same rankings in prevalence are observed. At this time, though, self-help organizations designed to address areas such as status and other addictions have grown. Niches in several new functional areas arose in the 1970s, and persist throughout subsequent decades. By the mid-1970s, one surprising pattern emerges: alcohol and drug addictions cease to be the second most prevalent functional area. Contrary to expectations that all areas of social life were being organized under the auspices of addictions from substance abuse to co-dependency (Kaminer 1992), the proportion of organizations devoted to these areas declined from 17 percent of the total in 1955 to 8 percent of the total in 2000.[7]

Instead, status or identity issues (e.g., gays and lesbians, men in nursing, gender dysphoria, and ethnicity) became the second largest organizing functional area, and remained so throughout the next twenty-five years. Over time, other functional areas emerge as well. Self-help organizations for disease and infections (e.g., American Hepatitis B Association, HIV Info Exchange and Support Group) have been around only since the 1980s. Yet, by the end of the century these types of organizations were prevalent. Based on the downward trend in density seen in fig. 3.1, we would predict that the proportion of disease and infections organizations would fall off in subsequent decades. However, if the HIV epidemic continues then there remains a need for these organizations.

One way to think about the distribution of organizations in functional areas is to imagine that equilibrium across niche areas would be observed if no functional area represented more than 5.5 percent of the total self-help population (100/18 areas = 5.5 percent). Given the actual distribution, we conclude that there are about three or four broad areas (i.e., relationships, status, eye/ears/nose/throat, disease, and infections) that dominate the distribution, while the remainder is evenly represented. Some areas, though, have only a few organizations representing them (i.e., mental illness, and skin and burns).

With respect to diversification, an interesting pattern emerges: initially, 11 of 18 functional areas are covered by self-help organizations. Several large fields dominate (i.e., relationship, alcohol and drug addictions, mental illness, and eye/ears/nose/throat). In the next twenty years, all 18 areas become organized. Except for one surprising shift, from alcohol and drug addiction groups to status groups, changes in the distribution of self-help functional areas were small but consistent in the direction of increasing diversification and equilibrium.

Specialists and Generalists

The previous discussion of diversification is one way of understanding how organizations take advantage of openings in resource space in order to exploit a niche. Resource-based frameworks detail the relationship between organizational strategies and organizational viability. In these models, organizations attempt to manage crowding in markets by targeting unique resource segments in an effort to reduce competition when different organizations converge on a single resource or production space (Carroll and Hannan 2000). By differentiating themselves from potential competitors, along a number of formal dimensions, organizations that do not enjoy scale advantages (e.g., usually newer or smaller organizations) can exploit variations in available resource space even when a market has attained a high degree of concentration. Concentration occurs when a few large (sometimes older), usually generalist, organizations monopolize a market. Consequently, environmental constraints induce organizational heterogeneity rather than homogeneity. Heterogeneity promotes organizational viability because market differentiation reduces competition through development of structures, routines, and practices that allow organizations to cultivate specialty niches.

In the self-help population, specialists and generalists are evenly distributed overall (48.2 percent and 51.8 percent, respectively). But the main interest is how do the dynamics of the population unfold over time? Table 3.2 details the shifting ratio of specialist and generalist self-help within and between subpopulations. I begin by sorting the organizations by prevalence of specialists and generalists in 1955. If resource partitioning takes place then the generalist populations will contract while specialists will grow. This has implications for who controls self-help, since generalist organizations can be driven

Table 3.2 Percent Yearly Active National Self-Help Organizations Using Specialist or Generalist Strategy in Each Subpopulation, 1955–2000

Organizational Subpopulations		1955	1965	1975	1985	1995	2000
Social Welfare	Specialist	50.0	54.0	45.7	41.2	34.3	34.5
	Generalist	20.0	22.0	23.3	26.0	25.6	24.7
Variance between years				$F = 41.34^{***}$			
Variance between groups				$F = 22.41^{**}$			
Alcohol and Drug Addiction		16.7	12.0	5.2	4.3	3.6	4.1
		0.0	0.0	2.6	1.9	2.8	2.4
Relationship		13.3	20.0	12.9	9.3	7.5	6.8
		10.0	8.0	7.8	5.9	4.7	5.1
Mental Illness		10.0	8.0	7.8	3.7	2.8	3.0
		3.3	4.0	0.0	1.2	3.1	2.7
Status		3.3	2.0	7.8	6.5	5.6	5.1
		0.0	2.0	2.6	4.6	4.2	4.1
Other Addictions		3.3	8.0	3.4	2.5	2.2	2.7
		0.0	0.0	0.9	1.5	1.1	0.7
Reproduction, Children		0.0	0.0	0.0	2.5	2.2	3.0
		3.3	2.0	2.6	2.8	2.5	2.4
Abuse, Violence		0.0	0.0	0.9	2.2	1.4	1.7
		0.0	0.0	2.6	2.5	1.9	2.0
Grief		0.0	0.0	4.3	4.6	4.2	4.1
		0.0	0.0	0.9	2.2	2.2	2.4
Physical Disability, Autism, Retardation		3.3	2.0	2.6	3.1	2.2	1.7
		0.0	4.0	2.6	3.1	2.5	2.4
Legal		0.0	2.0	0.9	2.5	2.5	2.4
		3.3	2.0	0.9	0.3	0.6	0.7
Medical	Specialist	10.0	10.0	10.3	7.1	12.0	11.1
	Generalist	20.0	14.0	20.7	25.7	28.1	29.7
Variance between years				$F = 4.26†$			
Variance between groups				$F = 7.30^{*}$			
Eye, Ears, Nose, Throat		6.7	6.0	5.2	3.1	3.1	3.0
		6.7	4.0	4.3	3.7	2.5	3.4
Cancer		3.3	2.0	0.9	0.3	0.3	0.3
		0.0	0.0	1.7	2.2	1.1	1.0
Neurology, Paraplegia		0.0	0.0	0.9	0.9	0.6	0.3
		6.7	6.0	7.8	7.7	9.2	9.5
Respiratory, Circulatory, Pulmonary		0.0	0.0	0.0	0.0	0.6	0.0
		6.7	2.0	1.7	1.5	1.7	1.4
Gastroenterology		0.0	2.0	0.9	0.9	1.4	1.7
		0.0	0.0	0.9	1.2	2.2	1.4
Disease, Infections		0.0	0.0	0.9	0.3	2.2	2.0
		0.0	2.0	2.6	2.8	2.2	2.7
Genetics, Metabolic Growth		0.0	0.0	0.0	0.6	2.2	2.4
		0.0	0.0	0.9	3.7	6.4	7.4
Skin, Burns, Reconstructive Surgery		0.0	0.0	1.7	0.9	1.7	1.4
		0.0	0.0	0.9	2.8	2.8	3.0
Number of Organizations (100 %)		30	50	116	323	359	296

*** p<.001; ** p<.01; * p<.05; † p<.10

by interests other than those of members with the focal condition. In fact, self-help displays a marked reversal of resource partitioning expectations. For self-help, the proportion of specialists dominates generalists until the late 1970s, at which point rising generalists overtake specialists. What accounts for this reversal? First, social welfare specialists decline markedly from a high of 50 percent in 1955 to a low of about 35 percent in 2000. Second, two interesting events parallel this decline in social welfare specialists: the proportion of medical specialist self-help is stable from 1955 to 2000 (at about 10 percent), but the proportion of medical generalists grows from 20 percent to about 30 percent. Not surprisingly, 60 percent of social welfare self-help organizations are specialists and 72 percent of medical self-help are generalists. Analysis of variance provides further support for these trends. Differences between declining specialist organizations and rising generalists are significant. Analysis of variance in over-time trends show that specialists decline significantly while the proportion of generalists grows, except for medical specialists, the proportion of which remains small and unchanging from 1955 through 2000.

Changes within subpopulations underlie these trends. Social welfare specialists in the areas of relationships, alcohol and drug addiction, and mental illness experienced precipitous declines over the history of the population, from double-digit to single-digit proportions. At the same time, medical generalists in neurology/paraplegia, genetics, and skin/burns/reconstructive surgery experienced gains that contribute to the slow but steady growth of medical generalist organizations.

While only more case-relevant analysis can uncover factors responsible for this reversal, it is likely that specialists and generalists in this population enjoy different economies of scale that do not correspond to the putative expectations that generalist organizations are necessarily "large generalists" and specialists are small. Pfeffer (1997) notes that in environments with uneven resource distributions, specialists might become larger than generalists, in which case expectations for concentration of large generalist organizations and growth of specialties would be reversed. Analyses to this effect (not shown) indicate that, at least throughout the first three decades of this population's history, self-help specialists were large relative to generalists. Finally, it may be that forty-five years is too short a time for generalist competition to yield a high degree of consolidation. I address this possibility in this discussion below.

Table 3.3 Specialist and Generalist Concentration: Proportion of Estimated Membership Held by Four Largest Active National Self-Help Organizations in Each Classification, 1955–2000[a]

Organizational Subpopulations		1955	1965	1975	1985	1995	2000
Population Shares							
	Specialist (n=4)	85.8	79.2	67.7	59.0	43.4	50.8
	Generalist (n=4)	11.9	9.2	9.2	10.7	19.2	16.4
Total membership		862,628	1,025,003	1,284,390	3,119,058	4,446,574	4,978,553
Variance between years				$F=5.77^*$			
Variance between groups				$F=33.61^{**}$			
Social Welfare Shares							
	Specialist (n=4)	91.8	87.1	80.4	71.3	53.4	61.5
	Generalist (n=4)	6.4	7.7	8.4	10.8	21.9	15.6
Social Welfare Membership		806,200	931,855	1,050,127	2,580,754	3,613,468	4,112,290
Variance between years				$F=4.35^\dagger$			
Variance between groups				$F=30.64^{**}$			
Medical Shares							
	Specialist (n=4)	0.2	62.5	53.6	24.6	10.7	8.5
	Generalist (n=4)	99.2	36.5	33.3	31.6	44.4	45.1
Medical Membership		56,428	93,148	234,263	538,304	833,106	866,263
Variance between years				$F=1.27$			
Variance between groups				$F=2.60$			
Number of Organizations		30	50	116	323	359	296

[a] Market share based on estimates of membership size
** p<.01; * p<.05; $\dagger$ p<.10

Self-Help Resource Partitioning

As we have seen, the question of resource partitioning in the self-help population is not a matter of the dominance of a few large generalists but how resources are distributed and concentrated among both specialists and generalists.

Table 3.3 provides a clearer picture of the extent to which concentration of resources occurs in the self-help population across several subtypes: specialists and generalists, and social welfare and medical self-help. Column proportions at selected time periods represent market share of membership held by the four largest organizations[8] in each of the indicated categories. For example, the four largest self-help *specialist* organizations (i.e., National Amputee Foundation, Taking Off Pounds Sensibly, Alcoholics Anonymous, and Narcotics Anonymous) controlled 85.8 percent of all population resources in 1955.[9] In contrast, large *generalists* (i.e., Al-Anon, Mended Hearts, Spinal Cord Injury Foundation, and the International Association of Larynectomees) held only 11.9 percent of member resources. Over time, trends reveal an interesting pattern: market share for specialists declines from 86 percent to 50 percent, and grows slightly for generalists, from 12 percent to 16 percent. The latter is consistent with predictions of a resource partitioning argument. Large generalists should dominate the sector through market capture. Were we to accidentally sample only medical generalists (last row), we might mistakenly infer support for resource partitioning: the four largest medical generalists controlled 45 percent of the market. Yet, overall (row 2), the largest self-help generalists controlled only 16 percent of the total market. The remainder was distributed mostly among specialists and a few other generalists. This pattern holds among social welfare generalists as well. The largest social welfare generalists captured only 16 percent of membership resources. As shown in the previous table, social welfare specialists dominate the self-help sector. Nevertheless, their influence declines over time from 92 percent of market share to 62 percent. Since partitioning theory focuses on explaining growth in the specialist population as a consequence of generalist consolidation, it is unclear what kind of competition occurs among specialists and whether *specialist* concentration follows from it. Specialization by definition seems to preclude concentration because each organization cultivates its own niche. Still, empirical findings in this population indicate that there are large specialists and these dominate the market in general, and among social welfare organizations. The final section explores reasons why this is so.

Conclusion

This chapter investigated resource diffusion underlying the evolution of self-help by examining founding and disbanding rates, diversification, and resource partitioning. Although the analyses in this section are exploratory, we learn that organizational ecological models of organizational dynamics are useful for understanding a variety of different kinds of organizational populations, including self-help. Specifically, the shape of growth and decline in self-help is comparable to that in other commercial populations ranging from newspapers, breweries, and insurance companies to social service agencies and women's movement organizations. In addition, by extending the basic tenets of resource partitioning to population-level analyses, it was possible to explore the anomaly that arises in most mature industries: how do specialist segments coexist in sectors dominated by a few large (generalist) enterprises? This is important because if the dynamics of diverse industries are comparable, explanatory mechanisms underlying any number of features of a particular system can be tested. In this case, while self-help population growth is comparable with commercial, bureaucratic and social movement organizations, the processes of resource partitioning are considerably dissimilar. Consequently, patterns underlying the latter need to be understood using a framework that illuminates the nuances of resource use in nonprofit sectors from that in commercial and bureaucratic ones. Some of this work has begun by looking at the organizational-level effects of market differentiation on viability (Archibald 2004).

Concerning market partitioning in the self-help population, I found that diversification occurs over the long run, with striking effects on the distribution of organizations throughout the population, and, subtle, but important effects on resource partitioning. Analyses of individual firms in studies of the beer industry (Carroll and Swaminathan 2000) and Dutch newspapers (Boone, Carroll, and Witteloostuijn 2002) show how market share becomes concentrated in the hands of a few of the largest firms (e.g., four enduring breweries end up with 80 percent market share, rising from just 10 percent). In contrast, the distribution across self-help subpopulations, and within social welfare and medical self-help, suggests that the domains most prominent at the beginning of the population's history, relationship/family, substance abuse, mental illness, and eye/ears/nose/throat remained so even as other specialty organizations and organizational subpopulations sprang up to form groups addressing additional problems and concerns.

Yet, if resource partitioning in the fashion indicated in most ecological work takes place in this population, then the generalist subpopulations within these functional niches should contract while specialists should grow. In fact, self-help displays a marked reversal in that the proportion of specialists dominates generalists until the late 1970s at which point rising generalist organizations overtake specialists (as shown in table 3.2). As in other industries, self-help generalists exercise economies of scale, dominate their competitors (whose failure rate increases), and eventually control large swaths of self-help. One consequence is that organizational membership and ownership of self-help becomes diluted by broader definitions of who can belong. What accounts for the reversal of specialists and generalists in the population? Forty-five years may be too short a time for generalist consolidation, and therefore both generalist concentration and specialist resurgence lie in the population's future. It is more likely, though, that the distribution of resources in the environment has important effects (Carroll and Hannan 2000; Pfeffer 1997) and that their use is contingent on whether professionals control access. For example, one type of ecological theory focuses on environmental conditions. Depending on variability of environmental change and the degree of uncertainty on decision makers' part about changes in the environment, either specialist or generalist organizations will be chosen as a strategy to deal with that uncertainty. The key prediction is that in certain environments (and in uncertain fine-grained ones) specialists will dominate generalists. This contrasts sharply with other theories that argue that uncertain environments always favor generalist organizations. Characterizing the degree of uncertainty in self-help environments and mapping it across subpopulations could help clarify why there is a reversal in the ratio of self-help specialists to generalists. In addition, the large discrepancy in market share between specialists and generalists, as well as the pattern of generalist dominance in medical subpopulations, suggests that environmental variability is critical in structuring these populations. This is an important extension of resource partitioning theory in that it explores how subpopulations of organizations emerge and control the field as a result of the processes of partitioning in markets.

The next step is to describe the particular socioeconomic, political, and organizational features of these population environments in order to answer the question why the distribution shifts in this particular way (e.g., perhaps legitimacy). I explore two important aspects of that question in the following chapters by examining the processes by which self-help gains legitimation and uses material resources and how these sustain its organizations. First, though, I explore the problems that self-help organizations face in achieving public recognition in order to understand how they acquire legitimacy to promote their causes.

4

Legitimation: The Paradox of Public Recognition of Self-Help

Examination of the dynamics of self-help in Chapter Three showed that organizational diversification unfolds as self-help evolves, with striking effects on the distribution of organizations throughout the population, and subtle but significant effects on how resources are divided among population members. What factors influence these dynamics? Social movement theories suggest that openings in the political system lead to the growth of movement organizations (Gamson and Meyer 1996; Meyer 2004; Meyer and Minkoff 2004) because organizers gain allies among elites in the political system. Organizational theories propose that the dynamics of organizational populations are a consequence of the distribution of cultural and material resources. Cultural legitimation (public recognition) and competition (for material resources) shape the trajectories of organizational populations by selecting the fittest groups for survival.[1] Legitimation and competition are important because they are the mechanisms underlying the institutionalization of self-help.

Self-help organizations face a number of obstacles in achieving public recognition and acquiring resources. These obstacles arise in four areas that are central to self-help's viability: medicine, academia, politics, and popular culture. Self-help, like other social movements and voluntary associations, is self-mandating. Self-mandating organizations are those able to generate their own legitimacy by appealing to an abstract moral authority based on rational voluntary participation. Members reinforce this precept through collective activities in which they share the goals of the group and donate resources to assure its survival. Yet, examination of case histories of self-help shows that like other social movements that challenge the authority of dominant interests, its advocates strive for mainstream recognition and acceptance as well. The two central questions that motivate the discussion of this issue are: how do self-help organizations acquire legitimacy to promote their causes, and, which sources are most important for recognition? In the next chapter, I address the related questions: Are some sources of legitimation more important than others, do these have differential effects on different types of self-help organizations, and how long do these last? But first it is important to understand why legitimation is necessary at all. To the extent that self-help organizations receive acknowledgment from external authorities, their ability to mobilize constituents and to garner resources is enhanced. The irony is that self-help takes an oppositional stance with regard to legitimating authorities. By examining several cases it becomes evident that despite its status as a challenger of the beliefs, practices and dominance of mainstream healthcare, self-help enjoys the recognition of the very sources it opposes.

In this chapter, I focus on the unique contribution medicine, academia, popular culture and politics make toward public recognition. Each source of recognition plays a significant role, but some groups depend more heavily on one source than on others. I first describe changes in mainstream healthcare that spurred the rise of the self-help movement. Next, I discuss several sources of legitimation that are helpful in understanding the movement. I apply these types of legitimation to four exemplary cases, Parents Anonymous (PA), the National Sudden Infant Death Syndrome Foundation (NSIDSF), Depression After Delivery (DAD), and National Alliance for the Mentally Ill (NAMI), to illustrate how self-help organizations acquire legitimacy from external sources. The first three of these organizations are parents' organizations for individuals involved in child abuse, infant death, and infanticide. NAMI was established by parents of deinstitutionalized mental patients. These four cases are typical of their sister organizations in how and where they seek legitimacy, but despite some similarities, PA, NSIDSF, DAD, and NAMI play to their own organizational strengths in how and where they seek it.

The Importance of Medical, Academic, Popular, and Political Recognition

Self-help organizations bring about social change in healthcare by implicitly and explicitly challenging the authority of dominant interests. To support and mobilize constituents, self-help organizers must demonstrate that their own mission, its organizations, and activities possess an equivalent, if not superior, moral justification. They must therefore acquire legitimacy as a means for engaging dominant interests in authority contests. Interestingly, the basis for doing so often derives in part from the same institutional sources that sustain the legitimacy of established interests themselves. Institutional sources of organizational legitimacy, as noted in Chapter Two, are the rules of the game governing what organizations can and cannot do (North 1990). Sports clubs in America do not typically run candidates for political office and political parties do not try to engage in professional sports contests. Institutional actors are those whose activities in a particular situation are consistent with the practices of that domain (e.g., in the case of healthcare, physicians and other medical professionals) while noninstitutional actors are self-help movement organizers and activists who seek change.

Social movement organizations acquire legitimacy to promote their own interests by creating an identity to win potential supporters. To create an identity, social movement organizers rearrange and transform familiar organizations for new purposes and in so doing, attempt to trade on the recognition and acceptance of already established practices. One strategic problem faced by organizers is how to extend the accepted practices in one area of social life to another. Some recent examples of the process can be observed in the civil rights, peace, and new age movements. The civil rights movement borrowed heavily on the conservative organizational and religious affiliations of its members to generate the moral underpinnings of a radical campaign devoted to the principles of freedom and justice aimed at undoing racial oppression. Similarly, the peace movement of the early 1980s drew on its members' affiliations with mainstream religious groups for validation of its mission (Wuthnow 1998). The appeal of civil rights and peace movement organizations came from their capacity to oppose dominant actors in a variety of institutional settings on ideological grounds that were familiar to constituents. In these cases, taken-for-granted beliefs and practices, such as the fundamental equality of all groups of people, were imported into diverse areas of social life (e.g., politics, education, market exchanges) in a way that dramatically transformed them. In a reversal of this strategy, proponents of alternative healthcare such as Deepak Chopra, Larry Dossey, Shakti Gawain, and Andrew Weil depend on the already established reputation of medical science to import religious and spiritual practices into the domain of modern medicine.

Social movement organizations generate legitimacy both from within the movement as well as acquire it from outside. These types of organizations are self-mandating and derive internal legitimacy insofar as they represent their constituents' interests. Their legitimacy increases when they achieve a measure of success in channeling those interests or effectively bringing about social change. Challengers acquire legitimacy from a number of audiences, some of whose interests they do not directly represent, such as bystander publics (McCarthy and Zald 1994). To acquire external legitimacy, organizers must span boundaries between constituents, such as civil rights supporters, who have an interest in a new set of beliefs and practices (e.g., racial and gender equality), and dominant actors (e.g., politicians, educators, employers) whose concerns are usually at odds with the emergence of the new way of life represented by the movement. Balancing conflicting interests is problematic as organizers juggle the need to mobilize constituents using a radical message of social transformation while relying on mainstream allies to provide access to system resources.

Needless to say, audiences for organizational activities, particularly socially disruptive ones, are not of one ideological orientation. Therefore, the ability of movement organizers to justify their cause may depend on convincing a variety of actors in a number of different ways of the appropriateness of movement activities. But the real challenge is gaining allies from social groups that are generally resistant to the cause. In order to gain a foothold in political arenas, some kind of recognition from entrenched interests is essential. Challengers need external validation in order to broaden the scope of their activities and gain access to resources. Yet seeking legitimation from dominant interests can compromise the principles of the enterprise since the process often results in creating alliances that risk fragmenting one's constituency. A particularly telling example is the anti-pornography movement of the early 1980s led by McKinnon-Dworkin, which generated immense strife among groups in the feminist movement. This strife was generated by the alliance between the anti-pornography faction of the left-leaning women's movement and the Christian far-right, which was also opposed to pornography on different grounds (Duggan and Hunter 1995).

Challenger organizations run the risk of alienating supporters in order to acquire external legitimacy. One consequence of seeking legitimation from dominant interests is cooptation, whereby challenger organizations exchange some of their self-generated (internal) legitimacy for mainstream (external) recognition and support. How and why this happens is of compelling interest to both organizations and social movement scholars because different social movement organizations will use different tactics and rely on different authorities for legitimation. To the extent that legitimacy is not settled, collective efforts to bring about social change, or merely to survive, may be futile.

Furthermore, as the movement gains legitimacy from its opponents through strategic affiliation, it runs the risk of being coopted itself. To explore this interesting struggle, I examine the ways in which medical, academic, popular, and political sources of legitimacy are acquired by the self-help movement.

How Legitimation Works

Social movement organizations are legitimate to the degree that their actions are "desirable, proper or appropriate within some socially constructed system of norms, values, beliefs and definitions" and that they are taken for granted (Suchman 1995:574). Social movements' legitimacy springs on the one hand from the capacity to channel their constituents' interests into appropriate activities. They are self-mandating and depend largely on their alignment with norms based on the right of individuals to form groups aimed at collective self-determination (Boli and Thomas 1999). Self-mandating organizations operate with reference to an abstract set of principles such as injustice, equality, freedom, human and civil rights, and democracy. On the other hand, social movement organizations require external support precisely to the extent that audiences must have some frame of reference for understanding these principles. A movement's justification for use of any particular set of tactics derives from legal and moral norms that are framed by social movement actors working back and forth across movement boundaries. For example, civil rights actors used the legal ambiguity surrounding the sit-in as a tactic to call attention to racial discrimination. As such, movement advocates must spend a good deal of effort shaping people's understanding of these norms by, in part, creating an organizational identity that embodies them.

Organizational Forms

In the process of creating new organizations, movement advocates must assemble resources, create new spaces, legitimate new forms, and integrate them with the prevailing institutional order (Rao, Morrill, and Zald 2000). The most efficient way to create new enterprises is simply to borrow the template of established forms. An established organizational form is a set of organizational characteristics, including structures, routines, and practices that are more or less permanently available for use. The easiest way to legitimate new forms is to trade on the already established legitimacy of permanent ones. Organizational forms, such as self-help, are embedded in clusters of practices and their justifications, which they use to present themselves as appropriate for the purposes at hand; their structures, routines, and practices must be consistent with individual and group experiences. For instance, some organizational forms may be "'appropriate for men' or 'appropriate for politics,' 'appropriate for rural communities' and so forth" (Clemens 1996:208).

The conceptual and moral acceptance of an organizational form can be determined by recognition among groups salient to an organization's functional role. For example, the peace movement of the 1980s was recognized as a legitimate political force by both civil and religious authorities because it was able to appeal to principles of fairness, nonviolence, and ideological tolerance that corresponded with beliefs underlying civic and religious institutions in Western polities (Wuthnow 1998). Similarly, recognition of self-help depends on external authorities who render judgment and confer legitimacy, corresponding to beliefs about the common good underlying Western civic institutions such as volunteerism, mutual aid, egalitarianism, and individual empowerment. Since self-help deals with healthcare issues, both the medical community at large and the professional health and human services community have a compelling interest in whether and how it meets their respective criteria of the common good.

Challenges to Mainstream Healthcare

While the medical community values its expert role in contributing to the common good, self-help contentiously engages medical authority over the basis of that expertise in the areas of healthcare. As noted previously, dramatic changes over a forty- to fifty-year period have marked the transformation of U.S. healthcare governance systems (see Starr 1982; Scott et al. 2000 for a discussion). The professional dominance of physicians gave way to greater federal involvement (e.g., in the form of Medicare and Medicaid programs) and the healthcare field became increasingly fragmented. In the early 1980s, deregulation shifted authority away from both physicians and the state to the private sector. All of these changes are currently reflected in decentralized governance structures and diversity of organizational forms in the healthcare sector. Gaps have appeared at the interstices of the sector, filled in by alternative forms ranging from herbalism to acupuncture to self-help support groups. While many new organizational forms seek newly freed resources from the splintered healthcare system, most are not positioned to contend with still-powerful medical professionals and other healthcare providers. Self-help cannot directly alter the hegemony of medical care or state intervention in health and human services. It can, however, influence how clients and practitioners see their role vis-à-vis one another through organizers' critical discourse, which targets the system of institutionalized medicine. Organizers' strategies, consistent with the culture of the movement, appear to arise from the oppositional *Zeitgeist* that developed out of new left/women's politics in the 1960s, 1970s, and 1980s. The critique offers a new natural and holistic paradigm in healthcare and denounces entrenched interests by advocating "traditional populist themes; cooperation and collective action; empowerment of both individual and social group; opposition to bureaucratization;... re-affirmation of basic core values related to the role of the community, neighborhood, ... self-reliance, anti-elitism and anti-expertism..." (Riessman and Bay 1992:37). Yet, for all of its vaunted opposition to professional elitism, including state intervention, self-help must remain linked to mainstream medical and health and human services professionals. To do otherwise would completely marginalize self-help practices. These professional sources, in medicine and academia, as well as politics, constitute the chief dimensions of self-help legitimation.

Sources of Self-Help Legitimation

Reputation serves as a source of authority and ultimately empowers organizations that display integrity and "good practice" (Parsons 1956:226–227). It may entail traits such as credibility, trustworthiness, and responsibility (Fombrun 1996). The reputation of an organization or the reputation of an organizational form is one dimension of legitimacy that shapes interorganizational resource exchanges. One important way to assess reputation is through recognition by other groups salient to an organization's social role.

Medical professionals, health and human services professionals, and affiliated academics generate recognition of self-help whether they oppose the principles of the movement—thereby affirming it by challenging the self-mandating feature of self-help—or support its principles, thereby demonstrating its mainstream appeal. For self-help, up through a certain period of time, opposition tended to be minimal.

After the mid-1980s, though, a number of books critical of it were published. A perusal of articles and books, ranging from the *Journal of the American Medical Association* to Ruggie's (2004) *Marginal to Mainstream: Alternative Healthcare in America*, shows that, nonetheless, positive discussion of self-help has been fairly widespread in the medical and academic literature.

Additional sources of recognition of self-help include the insurance industry, employee assistance programs, nonprofit foundations, workshops and conferences, the public at large, and state agencies (Powell 1994). Access to federal and state grant monies and favorable legislation signals to constituents and other audiences that political authorities recognize self-help as a burgeoning social institution. Consequently, representatives of self-help organizations appear before Congress and other legislative bodies to give expert testimony on medical and social welfare policy debates. Political authorities (in this case, members of congressional committees) generate legitimacy, based on their legal or regulatory authority. Even bureaucrats, such as the former Surgeon General Everett Koop, became movement allies. The Surgeon General's Workshop led thirteen federal agencies to initiate projects aimed at stimulating self-help (Illinois Self-Help Coalition 1997). In the following lengthy quote, indicating the breadth of Surgeon General Koop's interest in self-help, Koop acknowledges the oppositional character of self-help but supports its emergence (Margrab and Millar 1989: Proceedings of the Surgeon General's Conference March 13–15, 1989):

> In the fall of 1987, when on the campus of UCLA, I conducted a Surgeon General's Workshop on self-help and mutual aid. This movement arose because of the dissatisfaction of parents over certain aspects of health care delivery. This became a public movement arising from a perceived deficiency; but this was followed by unresolved turf problems between those who are engaged in self-help and those who deliver health care in a traditional way. The self-help groups tend to be somewhat hostile toward organized medicine, and doctors, particularly, appear to be suspicious of the more informal support groups. In spite of these attitudes, self-help groups have grown extensively and are also able to be very effective ... There are potential dangers associated with the self-help group; this form of care could become a hiding place for quacks and charlatans, and this could keep some people away from the mainstream of conventional health care. However, having worked with these groups now for more than three years, I think that eventually self-help will be the "other" health system in this country and that it will accept the burden of disease prevention and of health promotion

in the United States. If a partnership between the self-help groups and the doctors could be engineered, and the present hostility and suspicion allowed to dissipate, the result would be an outstanding combination of supportive and preventive care with diagnostic and therapeutic management. I believe there is a very important role for self help in the management of transitional care. I will direct appropriate individuals in my department to be a liaison between the Maternal and Child Health Office and the self-help leadership, and will keep you informed about developments.

Koop's edict clearly spells out the predicament in which self-help organizations find themselves. They are constituted by a disaffected public who must strive for external legitimacy, even as they challenge the latter's existing beliefs, norms and values, and seek to establish new ones. Several cases exemplify how Koop's idea of an alternative healthcare network play out in concrete terms.

Case Studies: Self-Help Legitimation

One of the important themes that I return to often in this book is that of conflict among self-help groups and professionals, even those groups who depend on professional guidance. As in most social science, the issue is not that any individual professional or professionally run group demonstrates oppositional relationships. Rather, it is the way in which the movement is portrayed by members and constituents that indicates a deeply skeptical ideological point of view. To a large extent, this skepticism arose from the cultural context in which self-help developed. Over the course of the 1960s and 1970s, an increasingly fragmented American counterculture aimed its critique of inequities in power at institutionalized medicine and healthcare. This critique paralleled growth of an alternative paradigm or ideology, if you like, in medicine and healthcare and the decline of physician hegemony. Activists, many with institutional homes in medicine and academia, acted as bridges between mainstream and alternative sectors in order to legitimate practices in the latter and help carry this paradigm forward. For self-help, entrepreneurial activities depended on portraying movements in terms of their links with traditional medical and academic systems of authority.

   In the following sections, I use descriptions of the early years of four self-help organizations, Parents Anonymous® Inc (PA), The

National SIDS Foundation (NSIDSF), the National Alliance for the Mentally Ill (NAMI), and Depression After Delivery (DAD) to illustrate how self-help organizations acquire legitimacy from external sources. Parents Anonymous, The National SIDS Foundation, National Alliance for the Mentally Ill, and Depression After Delivery exemplify the tenuous connection between challenger-based, do-it-yourself healthcare models and mainstream medicine. It will become apparent that in the following cases self-help organizers in each of the four domains of medicine, academia, and politics use their professional stature in an attempt to legitimate their broader causes, sometimes relying on established popular appeal, other times generating popular interest through articles and appearances in the media.

Child Abuse and Parents Anonymous

In the early 1960s, the syndrome of child abuse had putatively been discovered by an alliance of radiologists, pediatricians, and psychiatrists and publicized in a *Journal of the American Medical Association* article entitled "The Battered Child Syndrome" (in Pfohl 2003). This fueled a movement (called the reporting movement) aimed at uncovering and identifying cases of child abuse. The medical community, the first to confront the problem, along with a number of government agencies, the media, and voluntary groups (such as the League of Women Voters, the Daughters of the American Revolution, Council of Jewish Women, State Federation of Women's Clubs), formed the organizational nodes of the movement. When Parents Anonymous was founded later in the decade, medical attention, focusing on child abuse as an illness requiring psychiatric treatment, rather than legal punishment, was substantial.

Heralded by its board of directors as the nation's oldest child abuse prevention organization, Parents Anonymous® Inc. was founded in the late 1960s by Jolly K. and social worker Leonard Lieber. An organizational brochure (Parents Anonymous 2005)[2] describes the founding of Parents Anonymous through the "extraordinary efforts of Jolly K., a courageous single mother who sought help to create a safe and caring home for her family." The Parents Anonymous group consists of weekly mutual support meetings that provide a "safe, supportive, therapeutic environment" in which members learn to relate to their children in nonabusive ways. That the group emphasizes its "therapeutic" mission as a solution to child abuse is what constitutes the organization as alternative healthcare.

As with most mental health practices, members are encouraged to make behavioral changes that will foster positive family relationships. In addition, the organization serves as an advocate for the "creation and support of meaningful leadership roles for parents to ensure better outcomes for families." These various roles consist in providing a strong support network for parent members as well as technical assistance to community-based organizations and government agencies. Today, there are 267 accredited Parents Anonymous organizations and local affiliates that sponsor programs to assist members in transforming their relationships with their children. These programs are based on a model of "leadership-mutual support" that fights child abuse by eliminating parents' "risk factors such as unrealistic expectations, destructive attitudes, and harmful behaviors, while enhancing protective factors such as increased self-esteem, increased competencies and the provision of nurturing environment for parents and their children."

Institutional connections with famous individuals provide legitimacy for the organization. A board of directors governs a national organizational structure that includes an advisory council dominated by a number of public luminaries. The chair of the board of directors, Freddie Gardner, is himself a Parents Anonymous parent whose story was printed in a local newspaper. The advisory board of eleven members features eight TV industry-related personalities (James Avery, Dennis Franz, Bob Goen, Catherine Hicks, Craig Nelson, Phylicia Rashad, Jacklyn Zeman, and Lucy Johnson). It also includes a social worker, a child welfare foundation director, and a former State Commissioner of Human Services. The purpose of the advisory council is to extend public awareness about Parents Anonymous, and to promote its effectiveness. For community outreach, Parents Anonymous maintains a National Public Service Announcement program that functions as a tool for providing information to the public and professionals. Catherine Hicks and Phylicia Rashad both recorded service announcements for TV.

Based on a research profile published by the board of directors of Parents Anonymous, early studies (circa late 1970s) showed that the program was effective in reducing the number of violent behaviors, including verbal and physical abuse (see note 2). The newsletter goes on to report that the program serves as an effective strategy to reduce and eliminate the mistreatment of children. A review of the medical literature shows that a number of recent studies have analyzed the goals, functioning, and effectiveness of Parents Anonymous (Medline

2005).[3] This research has been published in journals such as *Child Abuse and Neglect, Journal of Psychosocial Nursing and Mental Health Services, Nursing Mirror, Child Welfare, Prevention and Human Services,* and *Social Casework.*

Institutional connections are highlighted in the organization's literature. Parents Anonymous leaders attend professional conferences, stage media events (such as awards ceremonies), appear on national radio and television shows, and provide testimony during congressional hearings. The research newsletter notes that Parents Anonymous was used as a benchmark program when Congress passed the Child Abuse Prevention and Treatment Act of 1996. In addition, the Office of Juvenile Justice and Delinquency Prevention promotes Parents Anonymous as one of the exemplars of the Model Family Strengthening Program. Linkages with other state programs include the program's visibility in reports of the U.S. Commission on Child and Family Welfare, and the Center for Substance Abuse Prevention. A Parents Anonymous leader, Jackie Ramirez, testified before the New Jersey Assembly Committee on Women, Families and Children and served as a member of a citizen's review panel overseeing the Division of Children and Family Services.

Annual awards provide more insight into the institutional connections that Parents Anonymous fosters. Reports from a PA brochure about the 2004 National Training Institute, which celebrated the 35th anniversary of Parents Anonymous, indicate that activities were geared toward developing members' advocacy skills. The newest training manuals used to teach members the goals of successful shared leadership are titled: *Shared Leadership in Action: Trainer's Manual* and *Shared Leadership in Action: Guidebook for Participants.* These manuals develop skills by which "parents and professionals build successful partnerships, share responsibilities, expertise and leadership, strengthen families and improve services and communities." Plenary talks at the conference were given by J. Robert Flores from the Office of Juvenile Justice and Delinquency Prevention; Dr. Susan Orr (Ph.D.), an Associate Commissioner of the Children's Bureau, U.S. Department of Health and Human Services; and, Aamie Bonsu, Public Health Advisor, Center for Substance Abuse Prevention, Substance Abuse and Mental Health Services Administration. Not surprisingly, PA's central argument in support of the critical social importance of child maltreatment, above and beyond the obvious yet unstated moral implications of it, is that it reduces a number of social problems such as "juvenile delinquency, crime, emotional and developmental problems, substance abuse, poor academic performance, homelessness and unemployment" (Parents Anonymous Research Profile Number 1, 2000:3).

Popular opinion and political connections are the two most visible sources of legitimation in these organizational advertisements. Research studies that seek to examine the effectiveness of Parents Anonymous in reducing child maltreatment highlight academic and professional recognition. Professional recognition is apparent in the founding of the organization under the auspices of Leonard Lieber, Jolly K.'s social worker. One area that seems less important is medical recognition. Although there are numerous publications in the medical literature (e.g., *Journal of Psychosocial Nursing and Mental Health, Child Abuse and Neglect*), Parent's Anonymous literature shows that it does not pursue recognition in this area very aggressively. Instead, it seeks to emphasize its linkages with state agencies, as well as media personalities.

First, media appearances call attention to, and highlight the tragic nature of domestic violence and the struggle to overcome mistreatment of children. Because child abuse had come to be defined as an illness rather than deviance, it had already attained the status of a health and human services problem.[4] Like other anonymous programs visible in the movement's early period (e.g., Alcoholics Anonymous, Narcotics Anonymous, and Al-Anon) the solution to the problem is embodied in the program's use of support groups aimed at parents whose characteristics define them as abusers or potential abusers of their children. From the standpoint of mobilizing resources and acquiring external recognition as authentic representatives of its constituency, Parents Anonymous receives thousands of inquiries, according to the organization's literature. By using the names and faces of well-know actors such as Dennis Franz and Craig Nelson, Parents Anonymous is able to normalize behavior that would otherwise be a source of shame and a good reason for avoiding any public exposure whatsoever, even showing up anonymously at a meeting. In this way, celebrity legitimates the organization and the media serves as a tool for recruiting members. It is also a means by which the purpose of the organization, its ability to monitor itself, and the proper fulfillment of its civic function (i.e., rehabilitating or at the least, managing, those who mistreat children) is kept in check.

Second, emphasis on the connection between Parents Anonymous and the state is crucial for the diffusion of the program's aims, including the passage of legislation related to child abuse and domestic violence. The importance of speakers from juvenile justice and child welfare programs at conferences explicitly frames the ramifications of the problem, but not the behavior per se, in social welfare and legal terms. No one needs to be persuaded of the legitimate authority of the state and its role in identifying child abuse and few people in this day and age of the medicalization of everyday life require much convincing that psychiatric medicine is the proper domain for treatment of an illness that results in battered children. From the point of view of the state, connections with voluntary groups such as Parents Anonymous implies a natural limit to state services. Parents Anonymous' connection to the Division of Child and Family Services lends it credence as an organization most likely to provide a continuation of those services if and when they reach their limit; that is, as a legitimate substitute for state support.

Third, research studies are an important source of recognition for Parents Anonymous, when they focus on the program's effectiveness, but also to the extent that they highlight the social and cultural ramifications of child abuse. Most of the studies cited by the organization focus on effectiveness, although independent sources identify a number of studies that mention the role of Parents Anonymous in providing support groups for individuals who abuse their children. For example, a 1987 article in *Child Abuse and Neglect* focuses on how professionals who discover child abuse cases can help clients accept professional services and seek support in groups such as Parents Anonymous. Other articles note the therapeutic benefits of attendance at meetings and encourage greater acceptance of the model.

It is probably not surprising that medical legitimation is lower on the list of organizational priorities than other sources. After all, radiologists and pediatricians discovered that their young patients needed treatment for trauma, and identified parents as the source of that trauma, setting up an antagonistic relationship (Pfohl 2003). A fairly large legitimation gap between medical professionals and Parents Anonymous might be expected, even though some of the medical literature recognizes its programs (e.g., *Journal of Psychosocial Nursing and Mental Health, Child Abuse and Neglect*). This is not the case with regard to the National Sudden Infant Death Syndrome Foundation. This organization, at one point headed by a medical doctor, was able to secure considerable recognition within the medical community and to advance its cause by taking advantage of this legitimation. That the group translated medical legitimation into political capital and became an important player in formulating legislation exemplifies an important way by which self-help becomes embedded in institutional life.

National Sudden Infant Death
Syndrome Foundation

Numerous articles and books have been written about Sudden Infant Death Syndrome, many address the role of self-help organizations in supporting parents of infants who die mysteriously in their cribs. The most prominent of these organizations was the Mark Addison Roe Foundation, later renamed the National Sudden Infant Death Syndrome Foundation (NSIDSF).[5] Pediatrician and former foundation president (1972–1977), Dr. Abraham Bergman (hereafter Bergman) recounts the medical dilemma surrounding the diagnostic puzzle of SIDS deaths, the history of the NSIDSF organization, its work, and the political struggles Bergman and others undertook to advance their cause. The title of Dr. Abraham Bergman's (1986) book, *The Discovery of Sudden Infant Death Syndrome: Lessons in the Practice of Political Medicine*, makes clear that the foundation used its growing medical prominence, in a number of forms, not least of which was the former president and founder's (Bergman) professional status, to gain political recognition and legislation aimed at addressing this problem. Academic and popular recognition soon followed.

To this day, there is still no clear diagnosis for the cause(s) of Sudden Infant Death Syndrome. The initial suspicion was that infants who died unexpectedly in their cribs in the first six months of their lives had suffocated or experienced some accident or trauma that led to death. However, forensic pathologists discredited this idea. Part of the dilemma was that coroners and pathologists had no standard procedure for conducting autopsies on babies, so it was impossible to gather data to test any particular hypothesis. Early autopsy research showed that some infants developed problems such as mastoiditis, heart disease, or pneumonia (Johnson and Hufbauer 2003). With rudimentary autopsies available, physicians expected to see a link between SIDS and respiratory disease (supplanting the suffocation theory). Parents were told to monitor their infants for respiratory abnormalities like troubled breathing. The media were instrumental in disseminating this change in diagnosis. *McCall's, Today's Health, The Child* and other magazines featured stories debunking the myth of smothered babies. A number of individuals who had lost infants to SIDS became active in promoting research and establishing support groups. One of the groups, the Mark Addison Roe Foundation, founded by the parents of a SIDS baby, Mark Addison Roe, provided meetings, financial grants, and an infrastructure for legal advocacy for its members. Other support groups, such as the Washington

Association for Sudden Infant Death Study, and the Guild for Infant Survival, arose to fill similar needs.

Access to professional and state resources grew in the 1970s as legislation was passed to address SIDS. Media accounts, such as an article in *Redbook* about the Mark Addison Roe Foundation, helped stimulate outreach and cement the political mission of SIDS groups. At the time, the National Institute of Child Health and Human Development was under considerable pressure from activists to allocate more research money specifically for the study of SIDS. The dilemma was that no uniform reporting system for SIDS deaths existed (sixteen different names were used to characterize it), making research problematic. This failure to agree on standards for reporting SIDS deaths was an object of contention for activists and state bureaucrats because estimates of SIDS death (around 10,000 a year according to Bergman's book) were argued to be too low to justify the allocation of federal money to cover research costs. According to Bergman, in 1971 the NSIDSF "forged a battle plan which took the form of a directed campaign at national, state, and local community levels," the goals of which were to promote research and help families. A combination of parents' advocacy, state intervention, and professional interests combined to transform SIDS from "an obscure medical mystery into an important medical research problem," (Johnson and Hufbauer 2003) which resulted in congressional hearings. Representatives of self-help groups were called to testify before Congress, and sympathetic TV and radio shows interviewed Bergman and others. Organizers, such as Bergman, and the founders of the Guild for Infant Survival, Saul and Sylvia Goldberg, were able to exploit these political proceedings. Success followed in 1974, when Congress passed the Sudden Infant Death Syndrome Act. This led to an exponential increase in money for research and considerable political legitimacy.

An ironic epilogue to the story is that some of the monies for research from the 1974 Act were intended to go toward counseling and state-run support groups for parents of SIDS infants. This had ramifications for local SIDS groups, since, as the state began to provide professional counselors located in special bereavement centers, parents' groups lost their autonomy and morale (Johnson and Hufbauer 2003). The movement nearly folded as the SIDS initiative came increasingly under state and professional authority.

Unlike Parents Anonymous, the medical profession and its political campaigns provides the most visible sources of legitimation in these accounts. Since the medical profession is embedded in academic organizations, academic recognition followed from these campaigns to the extent that organizers such as Bergman made their causes more widely known to the university community. As an organization with a physician at its helm whose expertise lay in pediatric trauma, the NSIDSF attained an enviable amount of recognition. First, media pleas for sympathy on local talk shows highlighted the mystery of the causes of SIDS. Since the diagnosis for SIDS was, and remains, unknown, medical professionals still maintain primary control of it. These medical professionals, however, are dependent on politicians who choose to allocate resources for its solution. Bergman's entrepreneurial work within the political system makes for an explicitly framed problem-solution set in medical and scientific terms that resonates strongly with the general perception of the dominance of the scientific paradigm. What could be more compelling than a set of scientific theories that posit an individual subjected to natural causes beyond his or her control, especially when the victim is an innocent baby? Causes, unknown or otherwise, can be organized under the rubric of scientific control. As noted previously, since medicine is one of the most easily recognized ways by which natural phenomena are controlled, people in modern societies are convinced of the legitimate authority of medicine, which increases demands for medical resources to address issues such as sudden infant death.

Activists like Bergman, and parents of SIDS babies like the Goldbergs and Roes, emphasized the political neglect of SIDS, not just its insidious nature and engaged in a campaign to mobilize self-help networks by setting up groups and foundations. Their demands were aimed at getting the political community to recognize the importance of the syndrome. Movement advocates raised moral concern over the failure of several government agencies to address a problem that was within their missions. They were so successful that their self-help groups became more formally structured and shed the one function that defined them as self-help: assisting families in overcoming their grief. With the passage of the Act in 1974, the NSIDSF became ever more focused on fundraising and maintaining its political capital. As Bergman notes, the Foundation came to near-dissolution because of its hard-line approach to fundraising at the expense of assisting families through support groups. This contains an important lesson: like many voluntary associations, the NSIDSF was too successful for it to continue pursuing the twin goals of promoting research and helping bereaved families. Given the state-run program set up to counsel bereaved parents, it was apparent that support groups could easily be taken over. The "near-dissolution" of the organization about which Bergman writes is really a successful transformation of the organization from one point of view and failure from another. NSIDSF exemplifies one route to institutionalization. Interestingly, it was the result of successful political contention that led to the death of one phase of the organization and the birth of another.

The next case, Depression After Delivery, also involves parents and children. Like Parents Anonymous, its origins lie in the nexus of crime and medicine. Unlike NSIDSF, however, its medical connections are more tenuous, and involve medicine and criminal justice, rather than medicine and politics.

Depression After Delivery

Depression After Delivery (DAD) is an organization devoted to the illness of postpartum depression. Founded in 1985 in Hamilton, New Jersey by Nancy Berchtold, who placed an article in a local newspaper, a support group was established to help new mothers cope with depression following childbirth. Taylor's (1996; hereafter Taylor) discussion of the early years of the group begins with a recapitulation of Glen Comitz' appearance on the *Phil Donahue Show* (airing May 20, 1986). Comitz appeared on Donahue's show to talk about the desperate psychological condition in which his wife, Sharon, had murdered their one-month-old son, Garret. Sharon Comitz was serving an eight- to twenty-year sentence at the time for drowning Garret in a local creek. Taylor notes that, up until the appearance of Glen Comitz on Donahue's show, the postpartum self-help campaign had been "just a support group." But on that morning a "full-fledged social movement" emerged. Others involved in the show that day, and presumably instrumental in the emergence of this social movement, were journalist and author, Carol Dix; Barbara Perry, a professor of psychiatry and former researcher for the National Institute of Mental Health; and an anonymous woman who had come to tell the story of her suffering from postpartum depression. The show elicited considerable media interest in the coming years. For example, in 1990, group members (Taylor 1996:61):

> made thirty-four appearances on nationally syndicated television programs and news broadcasts including *CBS Morning Show, Good Morning America*, the *Today Show, 20/20, Hour Magazine, Larry King Live…Geraldo*, the *Joan Rivers Show*, the *Morton Downey Jr. Show* and the *Sally Jesse Raphael Show*.

But the burgeoning popularity of this theme on talk shows belies the complex processes by which legitimation occurred. Three of these processes exist in Taylor's account of the transformation of Depression After Delivery from support group to movement organization. First, media appearances call attention to and highlight the intractable nature of depression as both an illness and social problem. What would otherwise have been a personal albeit tragic affair attains the status of a public healthcare issue because of emphasis on the social nature of the potential solution. The solution to the problem is embodied in the selection of guests: a doctor, an academic psychiatrist, and a fellow sufferer. While millions of viewers watched, the panel invited studio and home viewers to call in with accounts of their own experiences with postpartum depression and postpartum-induced psychosis. In this way, the prevalence of the illness is emphasized, heightening its seriousness, as well as its common nature, and raising moral concern over failure to prevent its devastating consequences. Second, Dr. Perry's appearance explicitly frames the problem in medical-scientific-secular terms rather than as an immoral or criminal act. As with SIDS, few people would question the legitimate authority of medicine to identify and treat the illness of postpartum depression. Not incidentally, the transformation of medical and academic legitimacy into popular support increases the viability of requests for additional attention and resources to address the problem.

Third, Taylor notes that Donahue emphasizes not only the medical nature of the illness, but its political neglect. She observes that what most viewers did not realize was that Donahue's guests were political advocates engaged in a campaign to mobilize self-help for postpartum women and to "demand that the medical establishment recognize their problems as a distinctive medical and psychiatric condition" (p.61). Here, movement advocates are engaged in raising moral concern over the failure of the political system to recognize the prominence of the medical-scientific paradigm, by taking remedial legal steps to address a problem that is clearly within its purview. Like other self-help organizations, in a relatively short period of time "one support group launched by a single woman blossomed into a national network of groups throughout the United States" (p.62). This kind of exponential growth characterizes the self-help movement itself and results from heightened visibility and legitimacy accompanying diffusion of groups across public space.

In an interesting juxtaposition, Dr. Perry's appearance notwithstanding, the medical profession has a long history of antagonism toward proponents of nontraditional medicine (such as depression-induced psychosis). For example, the American Medical Association (AMA) as recently as 1990 was still appealing a court ruling that held it in contempt of antitrust laws concerning the licensing of chiropractic medicine (Ruggie 2004). From the point of view of alternative medicine, the prospect of mainstreaming creates immense ambivalence. Medical recognition increases access to resources that help build organizations yet the medical establishment remains the chief opponent of complementary and alternative perspectives in the struggle for those resources. The very emergence of alternative healthcare practices stemmed from a growing skepticism toward the medical profession that it "might not deliver on its utopian promises and that within the medical establishment a new breed of practitioner was entering the ranks more concerned with financial profit than with humanitarian service" (Riessman and Carroll 1995:90). Yet, self-help activists seek allies among their antagonists in order to acquire legitimacy to promote their organizations.

Our last case takes up the issue of parents again, but this time focuses on those whose children are mentally ill. As we have seen with the three previous histories, the mission of these organizations evolves over time and with it the manner in which legitimacy operates. While the National Alliance for the Mentally Ill began as a parents' group, it experienced a dramatic transformation as its membership began to include those for whom the organization was established, the mentally ill themselves. In fact, with the increasing politicization of its members, it became a powerful advocate for changes in mental health policy.

National Alliance for the Mentally Ill (NAMI)

The National Alliance for the Mentally Ill (now called the National Alliance on Mental Illness) was founded in 1979 by families of patients discharged from mental institutions during the deinstitutionalization campaign of the 1970s (Katz 1993). Some of the constituent groups included Parents for Mental Recovery (founded in 1972), Parents of Adult Schizophrenics, Alliance for the Mentally Ill of Dade County, and the California Association of Families for the Mentally Disabled. In 1979, a University of Maryland professor studying support groups for those with mental illness helped organize a conference attended by 284 people representing 59 groups from 29 states (Katz 1993). Some of the money for the conference was provided by the Department of Education. The MacArthur Foundation donated $100,000 for a national office. Considerable political activity accompanied the founding of the national office and popular recognition followed increased access to the political system. In 1981, *Women's Day* reported favorably on NAMI and later that year the *New Yorker* serialized a story written about one woman's struggle to come to terms with schizophrenia. Books and movies with famous actors playing mentally unbalanced but heroic characters demystified mental illness and in some sense normalized its sufferers.

In 1983, a prominent psychiatrist, E. Fuller Torrey appeared on the Donahue Show to laud the work of NAMI, and turn over proceeds from his book on mental illness to the organization. Dr. Torrey's unconditional support for NAMI reflects the activities of an organizer engaged in boundary spanning between mainstream and alternative sectors. No less important than the doctors supporting persecuted mothers in Depression After Delivery, NAMI depends on medical professionals such as Torrey to promote its goals. This connection with the medical community is essential for sufferers of mental illness since most require its resources (e.g., medication, counseling, professionally regulated housing). The linkage with mainstream healthcare is so important, in fact, that while the majority of NAMI board members must be patients or families of patients, twenty-two psychiatrists sit on its advisory council.

As noted before, while hostility between actors pursuing mainstream and alternative practices creates grounds for contentious relationships, individuals cross boundaries and negotiate alliances in order to acquire resources and legitimacy for their causes. Because NAMI is structured to act as a social movement organization as well as a support group, its access to political resources such as those held by the Department of Education and the MacArthur Foundation is more developed than that of other self-help organizations. Cooperation between various groups with an interest in the mentally ill and local and state bureaucracies has been powerful enough to mobilize a large number of constituents and launch national campaigns with substantial financial success. Recognition in mainstream circles has been essential for NAMI's growth, which rose to 1200 local chapters by the beginning of the twenty-first century (NAMI 2005).[6]

The Challenge of Legitimation

Successful strategies to acquire legitimacy hinge on developing explicit connections with traditional medical and academic systems of authority and justifying these connections to a variety of audiences. Yet, audiences for organizational activities, particularly socially disruptive ones, are not of one ideological orientation. Therefore, the ability of movement activists to justify their cause may depend on convincing a variety of actors in a number of different ways of the appropriateness of movement activities. In the case of Parents Anonymous, the National SIDS Foundation, Depression After Delivery, and the National Alliance for the Mentally Ill, actors with multiple interests traverse mainstream healthcare and the complementary and alternative sector seeking recognition from established professionals. This creates a paradox in that self-help's critique of mainstream medicine, embedded in an ideological perspective based on the principle of autonomy from medical authority, has led to increased distrust and cynicism in those very sources of support. It is likely that given the division of labor in the medical profession (Scott et al. 2000) some occupational groups (e.g., psychologists, nurses, social workers, public officials, hospital administrators) are in conflict over their changing role in the medical system, and therefore tacitly support the ideology of complementary and alternative healthcare as a way to expand their professional jurisdiction. The Kansas City Self-Help Network is an example of expanding professional domains. It is a regional network (and not a self-help organization per se) established by a professional social worker whose personal circumstances made it necessary to create a regional network that links families with special needs to one another. As a support system, it provides the kind of interpersonal relationships based on mutual understanding and empathy that are considered necessary to cope with chronic illness and consistent with the ethos of self-help. Yet, it demonstrates how professional interests result in formalization and transformation of self-help into a social service. The following is a description of the network (Self-Help Network 2000):

> The Self-Help Network (SHN) was begun by Evelyn Middlestadt, a Wichita social worker who first came to understand self-help during many years spent working with adoptive families, especially those with special-needs children. Evelyn observed the special support and understanding that occurred when she brought together the parents of special-needs children who shared a common problem or concern. She found that people facing similar crises, experiences and life situations could provide an understanding and empathy that she, as a human service professional, could not provide.
>
> Ms. Middlestadt began to search for ways that she could provide the self-help support, which she observed with the adoptive families, to

a wider variety of problems. When she learned that some states had self-help clearinghouses, she used her personal savings to visit them and learn about their operations. At the same time, Evelyn decided to move her elderly mother into her home. In 1984, she quit her job to care for her mother. She also started the Self-Help Network. Her office was in her home and her desk was the corner of the kitchen table. She and her mother were the original staff members. Evelyn relied heavily on the services of volunteers to answer the phone, prepare mailings, create public awareness and maintain records. This assistance allowed Evelyn more time to train and consult with groups and to help others start new groups ... By 1985 the SHN had grown considerably, as had the demands on Evelyn. Fund-raising was a never ending struggle. Although Evelyn often did not take a salary to keep the Network operational, her hard work and perseverance began to pay off. Start-up funding for SHN activities and services were provided by a variety of individuals and foundations including The Coleman Company, Wiedemann Foundation, Koch Industries, Wesley Medical Center, and The Fourth National Charitable Trust. When her mother's health failed, Evelyn decided it was time to find a permanent home for the Network.

The home that she found for her organization was with Dr. Greg Meissen, professor of psychology at Wichita State University (WSU). The Network was transferred to the Department of Psychology at WSU, which agreed to provide some resources (but not funding). Greg Meissen became the Network's executive director during this time.

In this illustration, Meissen, a professional entrepreneur, acts as a bridge between mainstream healthcare and a burgeoning alternative sector organization. The network was ultimately transferred to an academic setting where resources were more readily available. Doing so provided an institutional framework for requesting funding for services, programs, and staff salaries. It is interesting to note how individual activists manage the tension between the ethos of autonomy of self-help and the requisites of legitimation that entail mainstream medical and academic recognition. While this case indicates a high degree of cooperation between professionals and self-help founders, the founder herself was actually a professional functioning in a private capacity. The emphases on the extent to which "volunteers" are the resources in the Self-Help Network and that the founder acted in a private capacity (along with her mother as staff assistant) shows how self-help tries to maintain its authenticity as a self-mandating enterprise.

Since self-help's legitimacy trades on recognition by audiences in already institutionalized fields such as medicine and politics, the struggle for legitimation yields an oppositional culture that tenuously spans mainstream institutions and its own alternative organizations and practices. Playing on divisions within mainstream healthcare while maintaining a challenger ethos makes strategic sense for self-help advocates since they succeed whether they are marginalized as outsiders, affirming their challenger status or recognized as insiders enhancing their established connections. Some of the legitimacy offered by medical and academic authorities is surely a function of boundary-spanning strategies and therefore a token of exchange by which some occupational groups try to dominate others by aligning themselves with self-help.

This raises two important questions: Are some sources of legitimation more important than others and how does differential support lead to taken-for-grantedness? To answer these questions I explore the broader consequences of public recognition as a series of trends in legitimation rates in the next chapter. The goal is to explain how temporal processes foster the growth of legitimation of self-help. While case studies show how activists work to establish connections between self-help and mainstream healthcare, investigation of longitudinal rates shows how different types of legitimation at the population level unfold over the evolution of the movement. Another way of thinking about these analyses is in terms of the diffusion of practices that are in the process of being institutionalized. Legitimation of self-help practices by medical, academic, popular, and political audiences is the mechanism by which institutionalization takes place. I investigate these mechanisms more thoroughly in the next chapter.

5

The Evolution of Public Recognition
and Its Consequences

Recognition by medical, academic, popular, and political sources uniquely contributes to the growth of self-help, and as the previous chapter indicated, different types of self-help groups rely on different combinations of authorities for legitimation. The discovery of child abuse as a medical syndrome (Parents Anonymous) was facilitated by radiologists and pediatricians. Sudden Infant Death Syndrome became a piece of federal legislation crafted by the National SIDS Foundation, which relied heavily on the political maneuvering of its organizers, while advocates for imprisoned mothers who had committed infanticide (Depression After Delivery) appealed for support from viewers of Donahue and other television shows. In these and other cases, the goals and ideas of self-help become a part of the common discourse as they are increasingly supported by legitimate authority and adopted by new groups. Naturally, other institutional authorities are important for the growth of self-help, but these four areas are the most potent. Case studies detailed how entrepreneurs work to establish connections between self-help and authorities in these domains. By limiting analysis to several instances of legitimation, however, the overall development of the movement remains unknown. Clearly, legitimation underlies the growth of diverse kinds of groups but the linkage between diffusion in Chapter Three and recognition in Chapter Four needs to be explicit. How does political maneuvering by, for instance, NSIDSF impact the founding and growth of other self-help organizations? This chapter examines longitudinal trends in the unique contributions medical, academic, popular, and political legitimation make to all of the different kinds of self-help groups.

First, I examine longitudinal changes in the average amount of legitimation provided by medical, academic, popular, and political audiences. This identifies the ways in which the four different sources of public recognition vary among themselves in the attention paid to self-help. Graphs show that recognition varies dramatically both between the different sources, and over the course of the forty-five years. Next, I analyze the trajectories public recognition takes in the four specialty groups: medical self-help, behavioral, psychological, and general purpose (status). These composite groups are derived from the eighteen-fold classification of self-help developed in Chapter Three. In analyses of the four specialty groups, I examine trends over the forty-five-year period and compare the sources of legitimation for each of the groups. The central issue is how important are the different kinds of authorities for each group. It is expected that recognition will be hardest to achieve from medical circles because of medicine's historically tight control over healthcare. It will also be harder to achieve from political authorities because their bureaucratic structures insulate them and are harder for outsiders to penetrate. It will be easiest to achieve in popular opinion, and only slightly more difficult among academics, some of whom work with self-help groups. The analyses indicate that not only are different kinds of authority important for different kinds of groups, but these influences vary over time as well. For example, political recognition is more important than medical, academic, and popular recognition for medical self-help groups such as Mended Hearts and Epilepsy Concern. In contrast, academic recognition is more important than the others for behavioral self-help groups such as Gamblers Anonymous. I discuss why this is so in a concluding section.

I also address the consequences of public recognition for the viability of self-help organizations. Although legitimation on an individual level may be worth obtaining, public recognition has consequences for the evolution of the population: it influences the extent to which self-help groups are formed. Using legitimation as a guideline, founders simply choose a common way of organizing to meet their goals since it is easier to build an organization that looks like other organizations. This process has a tipping point at which the degree of recognition accelerates the growth of the self-help population by fostering individual group formation. To make sense of this trend, we can examine the founding rates for the different specialty groups and compare these rates across the various sources of legitimation. These comparisons are based on simple measures of association that show the degree to which public recognition in one domain, for example, popular legitimation, influences the founding rates of different kinds of self-help organizations. Overall, the relationships between recognition and founding rates show striking differences between subgroups.

Measuring Specialty Groups

Recall that the data in the following analyses come from a newly created database that includes life histories of all 589 active national self-help organizations in the United States between 1955 and 2000. It contains year-by-year records that pertain to organizational founding date, organizational dissolution and changes in name, legitimation, and organizational resources. The database contains information on the four different types of self-help specialty groups (i.e., medical, behavioral, psychological, and general purpose), and four different types of legitimating authorities (i.e., medical, political, academic, and popular).

Four Types of Specialty Groups

Self-help organizations dwell in a variety of niches shaped by resource use and broader cultural norms about the collective identity of the chronically ill. Hence, there are a number of methods for examining the categorical dimensions of self-help. In Chapter Three, I divided the population into two main resource niches, social welfare and medical self-help, based on 1) provision of service and resource use and 2) definition of condition or illness. These two classes consist of a number of organizational specialty subgroups addressing a full range of conditions relevant to relationships (e.g., marriage, divorce, adoption, widowhood, family of addicts), alcohol and drug addiction, mental illness (e.g., coma, obsession-compulsion, emotional illness, depression), cancer, neurology (e.g., pain, sleep, stroke, paraplegia, head injury, fatigue) and respiratory, circulatory, and pulmonary illnesses, among other problems.

In this chapter and the next, I reorganize the eighteen subpopulations used in Chapter Three into a set of four types. Doing so makes analyses more manageable and addresses similarities between clusters of these groups in terms of group identity, the issues the group addresses, and resource use. This typology is also derived from Powell's (1987) classification:

- Medical disability organizations for the sick, injured, physically handicapped or impaired, and their family and friends (e.g., Autism Network International, National Amputees Foundation, Alliance for Lung Cancer Advocacy, Support and Education)
- Behavioral organizations that help members change some problematic behavior (e.g., Alcoholics Anonymous, Rational Recovery, Debtors Anonymous, Nicotine Anonymous) or behavioral support organizations that provide support to those whose partners, relatives, or friends engage in some problematic behavior (e.g., Al-Anon, Alateen, Co-Dependents Anonymous)
- Special-purpose psychological organizations that address a range of problems from grief, loss, and abuse to anxiety (e.g., The Compassionate Friends)
- General-purpose psychological organizations that address stigmatized statuses (e.g., American Assembly of Men in Nursing, National Federation of Parents and Friends of Gays).

We can think about these groups in terms of the stigma attached to their conditions and the system responsible for managing them. Classifying self-help into these specialty groups clarifies the link between members' conditions, their stigma, and the authorities who preside over these domains. Still, it is not entirely clear which source of legitimation works best for members of which group. For example, although the medical profession has been slow to divest itself of the prerogatives of its control over the domain of healthcare (Goldstein 1992; Weitz 2001), the discussion of self-help has been fairly widespread in the medical literature. Likewise, academic audiences with an interest in self-help include social workers, public administrators, and psychologists who publish articles about self-help groups and their members. The following analyses will uncover more of these relationships and test whether they influence formation of other self-help organizations. Table 5.1 defines the various measures used to analyze these relationships in the following graphs and tables.

Table **5.1**   Variable Definitions for Founding Rates and Legitimation. National Self-Help/Mutual-Aid Organizations, 1955–2000

Measures	Definitions
Organizational Founding Rate	Number of organizations formed in a year
Legitimation	
Medical Legitimation	References in medical literature
Academic Legitimation	References in academic literature
Popular legitimation	References in the *New York Times*
Political Legitimation	Congressional appearances and testimony
Resource Niches	
Medical	Self-help organizations focusing on
Behavioral	medical, behavioral, psychological,
Psychological	and general conditions
General-Status	

Measuring Legitimation: Self-Help Database Sources

Medical professionals, academics, popular opinion leaders, and politicians are institutional authorities who contribute to self-help's success through their recognition of it. Quantifying these sources of legitimation makes it easier to investigate patterns by which the movement is regarded by them.

In the quantitative analyses of legitimation rates, medical legitimation is measured by counts of articles at each time period referencing each of the 589 self-help organizations from 1955–2000. Articles were compiled by the National Library of Medicine's *Index Medicus-Medline*. This index contains articles in 4,300 periodicals ranging from the *New England Journal of Medicine, Journal of the American Medical Association, and International Journal of Psychiatric Medicine, to the Journal of Consulting Clinical Psychology*. Locating these records involved a search by name of each self-help organization over the period of its existence. For some organizations such as Alateen (circa 1957), the search covered a forty-three-year period. For other organizations, such as Depression After Delivery (circa 1985), the task involved a seventeen-year search. I measure academic recognition of self-help in the same way by counting articles contained in journals in the *Sociological* and *Psychological Abstracts*. These databases provide access to 3,800 scholarly journals, including the *American Sociological Review, American Journal of Sociology, Psychological Bulletin, Psychological Assessment, and Journal of Community Psychology*.

In addition, I assess popular recognition of self-help using counts of articles from the *New York Times*. Media coverage of the entire forty-five-year period required access to a journal that retained records of its articles over that time period, while also providing electronic access to search for almost six hundred names multiplied by forty-five years. The *New York Times* was well-suited to this purpose. To the extent that a newspaper such as the *Times* publishes major stories and reports, and identifies meeting times and places, self-help achieves a great deal of popular support.

Lastly, members of congressional committees generate political legitimation for self-help through the relationships and alliances they develop. Self-help activists meet with politicians, appear before Congress and other legislative bodies, give expert testimony on medical and social welfare policy debates, lobby for fiscal support, and seek legal reform. Political authorities can then generate political legitimation for self-help organizations. I measure political legitimation by references to appearances and testimony in congressional hearings of each of the 589 self-help organizations active at one time or another in the United States. The task was facilitated by *Congressional Universe/Congressional Information Services*. The *CIS* subject index includes all regularly produced publications including hearings, testimony, and reports of such political bodies as the House Interior and Insular Affairs Committee, Department of Labor, Department of Health and Human Services, Department of Education, and Related Agencies for Appropriations.[1]

In each of these four measures of legitimation, the question of whether or not self-help received a favorable assessment arises. In constructing this dataset, I examined journal articles, newspaper accounts, and congressional reports closely to gauge the degree to which articles were favorable to self-help or not. Close inspection of articles showed that references tended to be either neutral (e.g., reporting the outcome of a study) or positive (e.g., praise for an organization's skill in serving a marginalized population such as the mentally ill). The *New York Times,* for instance, operating under the principle of fair and balanced coverage, tended to promote self-help even though it incorporated the occasional dissenting voice in its stories.[2] Individual organizations usually referred to these opportunities for publicity in their own autobiographical histories. These histories typically referenced journal articles, newspaper accounts, and congressional testimony as a sign of the efficacy, importance, and legitimacy of the organization. For example, the headline "Troubled Millions Heed Call of Self-Help Groups" in the *New York Times* July 16, 1988, typifies articles in the popular press publicizing the availability of thousands of support groups across America in the 1980s and 1990s. Nonetheless, skeptical accounts of self-help do appear, largely in books published in the late 1980s.[3]

The Importance of Different Sources of Legitimation

Some key research sheds light on the three questions concerning legitimation that this chapter addresses. Organizational ecology and neoinstitutional theories suggest that when an organizational form becomes prevalent, it achieves legitimacy because common use indicates acceptance, even taken-for-grantedness (Carroll and Hannan 2000; Scott 2003). When we ask, "What are the long-term trends in public recognition of self-help?," the answer is that, today, self-help is in fact largely taken for granted. Self-help has become a part of our common vocabulary, our technology for organizing support groups (e.g., twelve-step groups), and even our laws (e.g., SIDS Act of 1974, the Disability Discrimination Act of 1995). But what trends shaped this process, which different kinds of authorities were important for the growth of different self-help organizations, and how might we view the effects of various authorities on the formation of self-help movement organizations?

Bear in mind that as a population of organizations becomes increasingly legitimate, more instances of that form emerge, and vice versa, so that population growth spirals upward. In a short period of time moderately large increases in legitimation lead to exponential increases in organizational foundings. Legitimation boosts self-help because it reduces costs of organizing as the form becomes successful at what it does. The magnitude of this reciprocal process varies depending on how tightly controlled a sector is, by different sources of institutional authority and power. Meyer (2004) and Clemens (1996) argue that organizations are integrated to a greater or lesser degree into a variety of institutional sectors characterized by the extent to which contexts are exclusive and foster actor autonomy. Consider how medicine and politics, academia and popular culture influence self-help formation. The authority structure over organizations situated in the domain of medicine produces tightly integrated networks because mainstream medicine depends on centralized professional control of healthcare services. Professional control of healthcare is based on a hierarchical system of formal structures ranging from medical schools and health-care facilities to professional bodies such as the American Medical Association. It is expected, then, that authority in medical contexts will be more tightly coupled and will reproduce professional hege-mony by limiting the formation of organizations that contest that dominance. More institutional control results in fewer sources of legitimation and greater barriers to self-help formation. The domain of politics is no less formalized but its authority structure is less cen-tralized with respect to social movement organizations such as self-help. The other two sources of legitimation for self-help, academia and popular opinion, are even less structured. Legitimation comes quickly and readily in popular culture. Stories in the press laud the civic good created by self-help groups and their proliferation follows.

Self-help organizations can achieve legitimation consistent with the level of control of their authority structures. Medicine is the most difficult to penetrate, followed by political institutions and academia and then the popular press. In the following section, I investigate these relationships using graphs and determine whether this is so.

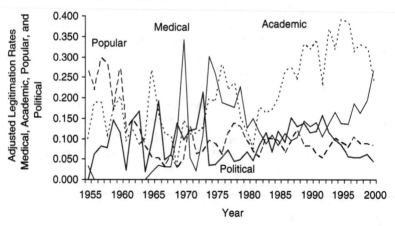

Figure 5.1 Adjusted Legitimation Rates for Self-Help Organizations, 1955–2000

Public Recognition: Evidence
from Self-Help Data

Trends in fig. 5.1 depict the unfolding legitimation of self-help over its forty-five-year history. Categorizing the evolutionary periods into fifteen-year aggregates, 1955–1970 represents the emergence or youth of the population; 1970–1985 represents self-help's adolescence; and 1985–2000 the population's maturity. Fig. 5.1 shows the adjusted legitimation rates for self-help for the four public domains. Examining these rates, it is obvious that legitimation varies widely between domains.[4]

In the earlier years, all adjusted legitimation rates show similar peaked increases and decreases through the mid-1970s. The jagged peaks of the earlier periods suggest that taking account of population size, legitimation varies widely, with averages spiking and declining regularly until the 1970s. At this time, medical and academic legitimation turn upward and stabilization occurs for popular and political legitimation. Popular legitimation shows an exceptional pre-1970s pattern: it descends from a high in the 1950s through the late 1960s. Then it remains relatively flat throughout the end of the century. These trends imply that with fewer self-help organizations around, through the early 1970s, recognition by medical, academic, and political authorities was stable, at which point it rose slightly for political recognition and considerably for medical and academic sources. In contrast, popular legitimation experiences a marked decline between the emergent and adolescent stages in the population's history, an unexpected drop from which it never recovers.

Overall, medical legitimation and to a lesser extent, academic legitimation, peaked in the 1970s, declined, and then rose from the 1980s through the end of the century. Why does there seem to be a change in linear trends, at least in the adjusted numbers in fig. 5.1, around the 1970s? Self-help advocates' arguments, based largely on cultural perceptions at the time, claim that the phenomenon took off during the 1970s because of disillusionment with mainstream healthcare (Katz 1993). With organizational data at hand, we can be more systematic in identifying what happened and when. Clearly, political and popular legitimation do not contribute to legitimacy in the 1970s. On the other hand, medical and academic domains show a marked increase in recognition of self-help. These data provide mixed support for self-help proponents' suggestion that self-help "took off"—became more legitimate—during the 1970s. Organizational ecologists would argue that legitimation, typically strong during a population's emergent phase, may stabilize as the population becomes more or less generally accepted (Hannan 1998). Occasionally, populations experience resurgence marked by growth in legitimation during the later stages. Interestingly, medical and academic legitimation do not continually rise to equilibrium. Both peak in the 1970s, decline, and experience a resurgence in the 1980s. To understand what is happening here we can briefly preview the counterpart to legitimation, competition. Competition for resources erodes gains made by legitimation. Analysis of competition in the next chapter shows that it rises consistently beginning in the late 1960s and early 1970s. Rising competition during the 1970s and declining political and popular legitimation suggests that the two operate in tandem: legitimation and competition rise with the increasing number of organizations but competition for diminishing resources means that fewer are available for new organizations.

In contrast, political legitimacy never reaches equilibrium and moves in a cyclical fashion over time, while popular legitimation reaches equilibrium only after a downward trend. Political recognition passes through several high and low cycles. These cycles can be explained in that state support of mainstream and alternative healthcare and human services has always been divided. On the one hand, the National Institutes of Health (NIH) encompass several divisions funding complementary and alternative medical research. This includes the National Center for Complementary and Alternative Medicine that began with a budget of $2 million in 1992 and in 2002 had a budget of $104.6 million. A number of universities are funded by this budget including Columbia, Harvard, and Stanford (Ruggie 2004). On the other hand, The Omnibus Reconciliation Act (OBRA) of 1981 began the devolution of public policy by reducing federal spending for public programs and the consolidation of social welfare programs. As noted earlier, in spite of welfare state devolution, federal healthcare spending grew rather than declined during devolution in the 1980s and 1990s (Smith and Lipsky 1993). While it was argued that reduction in governmental involvement in health and human services would increase private entrepreneurial activities, Chapter Three shows that population founding rates began to decline rather than grow during the 1980s. Moreover, Surgeon General Everett Koop's 1987 recognition of self-help followed reduction of federal spending for public programs and the consolidation of social welfare programs under OBRA 1981. The drop in political legitimation rates following Koop's 1987 Workshop lends some credence to advocates' claims that state support was largely a rhetorical strategy. State support of self-help seems therefore to be ambivalent at best.

As noted, the pre-1970s adjusted rates for medical, academic, and political legitimation are very different from popular rates. Why is popular legitimation high to begin with while medical, academic, and political sources begin low and then increase? The press is likely to have been much more attuned initially to self-help relative to the size of the phenomenon than medical, academic, or political sources because its standards for observing and explaining social phenomena are less stringent than those of the sciences. Medical recognition, academic legitimacy, and political support are probably harder to come by because journal articles and Congressional appearances are based on research studies (in the former case), and political influence (in the latter case) which makes for more rigorous selection criteria. For example, stories in the press in the 1980s, when self-help reached its largest size, announced that "Group Lends Helping Hand in Adoptions" (*New York Times*, April 1987). Many of these articles were filled with glowing recognition of the individual and civic good provided by voluntary community-based groups such as Compassionate Friends, AA, and Friends in Adoption. They were "news." The medical counterpart to these advertisements for self-help can be seen in a research study conducted in May 1994 and published in the *Journal of the American Optometric Association* (Maino et al. 1994). Its headlines were less dramatic than the announcement of the rising deluge of millions of self-help constituents. Instead, it pointedly explored "Ocular Manifestations of Sotos Syndrome" (and the role of Sotos support groups). Much of the recognition and legitimation in medical and academic domains, as evidenced in the cases above, entails appraisal, proper categorization or recategorization, and analysis of outcomes of a serious illness, stigma, or problem. For instance, the *International Journal of Psychiatric Medicine* (Peindl et al. 1995) examined the "Effects of Postpartum Depression on Family Planning" in 1995 (referencing DAD) and the *Journal of Consulting Clinical Psychology* (Yeaton 1994) was interested in "The Development and Assessment of Valid Measures of Service Delivery to Enhance Inference in Outcome-Based Research" by "Measuring Attendance at [DAD] Self-Help Group Meetings." Political legitimation has similar exacting standards. Political appearances are likely to involve a much higher expectation of self-help accountability than stories in the press because group spokespersons become experts providing legal testimony before Congressional committees such as the House Committee on Appropriations, the Committee on Aging, and the Committee on Commerce.

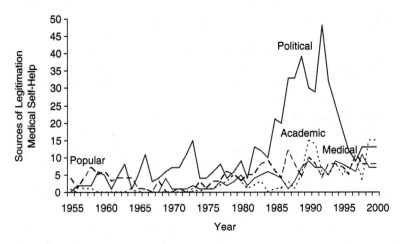

Figure 5.2-A   Legitimation Rates for Medical Self-Help Organizations, 1955–2000

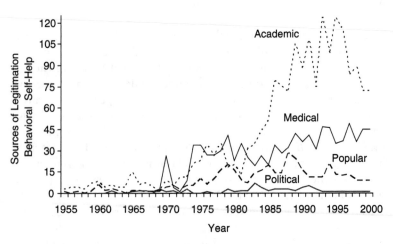

Figure 5.2-B   Legitimation Rates for Behavioral Self-Help Organizations, 1955–2000

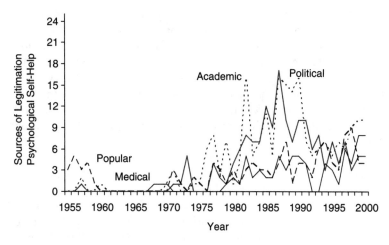

Figure 5.2-C Legitimation Rates for Psychological Self-Help Organizations, 1955–2000

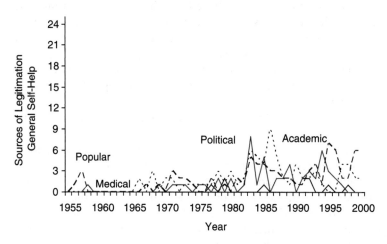

Figure 5.2-D Legitimation Rates for General Purpose Self-Help Organizations, 1955–2000

Public Authorities and Self-Help: How Trends Affect Specialty Subgroups

Like fig. 5.1, the four graphs in figs. 5.2 continue to depict the burgeoning public recognition of the self-help subspecialties over its forty-five-year history. The graphs in this figure show the relationship among the different sources of public recognition and medical, behavioral, psychological, and general specialty groups.[5] As I emphasized in the discussion of fig. 5.1, the four sources of legitimation show a remarkable variation over the history of the population. The central question these figures address is: where do different types of self-help get their legitimacy? On the basis of the four graphs in total, the answer to the question is that different kinds of authority are important for different kinds of groups. In other words, legitimation is differentially allocated among groups. Later, we will see how differential allocation of recognition influences the growth of these groups in interesting ways. Differences can be highlighted by comparing the trajectories within and between subspecialties. For medical self-help, the graph in fig. 5.2-A shows that this type of group derives its legitimation from political authorities, especially during its mature years, 1985–2000. During the early and middle years, political legitimation dominates medical, academic, and popular recognition. But then it accelerates dramatically in 1985. We would have supposed that medical authorities would have been the key players in medical self-help, such as the Myasthenia Gravis Foundation, Mended Hearts, or Epilepsy Concern. However, self-help's challenge to mainstream medical hegemony is met by resistance on the part of medical professionals. The marked decline in political legitimation in the late 1990s indicates that fewer medical organizations were being called to testify before Congress. This may be due either to a slackening of interest or because medical self-help organizations were disappearing, and thus, there were fewer to testify.

Fig. 5.2-B shows a remarkably different relationship. For behavioral self-help, academic recognition predominates, especially during the mature phase of the movement. Where political recognition drove medical self-help, academic recognition is far and away the legitimating source of authority for behavioral groups such as Al-Anon and Pills Anonymous. Political recognition, in fact, had a marginal relationship with the behavioral groups. This is not surprising because this type of organization includes the anonymous twelve-step groups whose stated mission precludes involvement in political affairs per se. Another interesting pattern emerges for the behavioral groups: medical legitimation maintains a fairly steady level beginning around the middle years and rising only very slowly through maturity. This trend indicates that medicine's influence on behavioral groups is tentative at best. It is higher for behavioral groups, though, than for medical, psychological, and general-purpose groups. This is probably due to medical recognition of drug and alcohol addiction as a disease, since these groups make up the majority of the behavioral subspecialty area (AA World Services 2005).

Figs. 5.2-C and 5.2-D show the relationship between the four legitimating authorities and psychological and general-purpose groups. Again, academic and political legitimation reign during the mature phase but neither is consistently dominant. Each rises and falls to a similar degree between the 1970s and 1990s, indicating that academic and political recognition are of overwhelming importance for psychological and general-purpose groups. Another interesting similarity between the two types of groups is that popular recognition rises in the mid-1990s to overtake a declining political trend toward the end of the decade. How do these trends influence growth in the size of the population? The final section investigates this issue.

Table 5.2 Coefficients Measuring the Strength of Association between Legitimation and Founding Rates

Sources of Legitimation	Medical Founding Rate[a]	Behavioral Founding Rate	Psychological Founding Rate	General Founding Rate
Medicine	0.243	0.231	0.021	0.157
Academia	0.119	−0.051	0.252*	0.296*
Popular Press	0.281*	0.375*	−0.136	−0.046
Political	0.284*	0.211	0.311*	0.082

[a]Starred * numbers indicate .05 level of significance or less

Predicting Self-Help Formation

Public Authorities and Self-Help: How Does Legitimation Influence Founding Rates?

Having determined that different public authorities are important for different self-help groups, how does differential recognition by public authorities affect the formation of medical, behavioral, psychological, and general self-help? Recall that legitimation of self-help reduces the costs of foundings and make it easier for organizers to start their own self-help groups because it provides a template for organizing. I assess the influence of legitimation on organizational formation by using a measure of association that captures the strength of fit that each type of authority has with the founding rates for the different groups.

These associations or correlations are shown in table 5.2 and they should approximate the patterns discovered in the relationships in the graphs above. As discussed in Chapter Three, the organizational founding rate is the number of organizations established during any one of the forty-five years of the population's existence. The founding rate is the number of new organizations started *per year*. Organizational ecology predicts that as legitimation rises from year to year, so too will the rate at which self-help organizations are founded. To make the causal relationship more plausible, legitimation is measured prior to the founding rate by a year so as to eliminate the possibility of reverse causation. Naturally, there will be other factors that influence the rate at which self-help organizations are being formed but it is essential to the topic of this book to establish whether legitimation is one of them.

Two criteria will help explain the correlations in table 5.2. Any coefficient from .10 through .30 indicates a small but increasingly meaningful relationship, and any larger than .30 through .50 indicates a moderate-sized one. Also, correlations that are starred indicate that the relationship is significantly different from 0 (based on the conventional .05 level of significance) to warrant our attention.

Given trends in the fig. 5.1-A, it is not surprising that table 5.2 shows that political authorities have a significantly powerful influence on the medical founding rate, as does the popular press. Because we have lagged legitimation, and made the verbal argument for a link between legitimation and founding rates, it can be argued that increases in political legitimation foster medical self-help founding rates.[6] The table suggests that medical authorities are unlikely to support alternative medical practices that threaten their hegemony, while politicians and the press have little to lose by supporting them. Moreover, the influence of academic recognition on the medical self-help founding rate is trivial.

Having learned that the behavioral groups receive a disproportionate amount of academic recognition, it would not be surprising to see this reflected in behavioral founding rates. Yet, the only significant relationship is with popular legitimation (0.375). Here, there exists a moderately strong relationship between increases in popular acclaim and the growth in behavioral self-help. Academic recognition, burgeoning in the adolescent and mature phases of self-help's evolution, is not related to the founding rate at all (the fact that the coefficient is negative is largely a statistical artifact). This contrasts with the effects of academic recognition on the founding rate for psychological groups and general-purpose groups, which has a significant influence. Organizations in psychological and general-purpose specialties, such as Parents Anonymous (circa 1971) and The Compassionate Friends (circa 1977) are given the impetus to form based on prior academic recognition of their precursors, say, Recovery, Inc. (circa 1937) or La Leche League International (circa 1956). The direct connection is not an obvious one until we remember that it is largely the organizational *form*, the beliefs and practices of self-help, that becomes the template for later groups. These findings indicate that legitimation of one set of groups under the auspices of one authority translates into a greater likelihood of the emergence of other groups, in that class of organizations, at a later date.

Conclusion

This chapter shows that different sources of legitimation will have different effects on groups and their founding rates depending on the specialty niche. Where it might have been expected that medical groups such as Reach to Recovery or Associated Blind would rely exclusively on mainstream medicine and the healthcare industry for justification, this is not so, largely because mainstream medicine remains hostile to alternative practices. We saw in Chapter Four, however, that some individual medical professionals support self-help. Still, it is surprising that medical self-help itself is indebted to political authorities for recognition. In contrast, behavioral groups such as Gamblers Anonymous and Al-Anon find legitimation in academic circles, rather than in medical or political communities. The conclusion is that legitimating authority is not a single generic entity but a varied set of organizations, rules, and practices governing recognition of self-help groups. Recognition from medical authorities barely mattered when it came to founding new self-help organizations in any of the four niches. Yet, the extent to which groups in certain niches acquired political capital had an effect on the likelihood of organizations forming in that niche. That popular legitimation served to promote self-help formation, but only for groups occupying the medical and behavioral niches, begs the question as to why for these niches and not the other two? Before we explore the issue in the concluding chapter, it is important to note that the point of investigating public recognition of self-help is not just that it indicates the extent to which it has become a popular method for engaging in healthcare support, although this seems to be so, but that legitimation serves as a mechanism that drives the growth and, ultimately, the institutionalization of self-help.

Legitimation's effect on organizational formation provides us with an alternate view of how organizational founding rates rise, in contrast to explanations that rely on the sole influence of individuals' enterprising activity and rational-choice behavior generated by unmet needs. While legitimation may turn out to carry less causal weight than suggested here (a multi-causal explanation is probably more likely), its importance in elevating one template for organizing collective action is supported by the dynamics of population growth, as shown in the graphs and tables in this chapter. But self-help also experienced a decline brought about by decreasing founding rates and increasing dissolution. What mechanisms account for these dynamics? In the next chapter, I examine how competition for the diminishing resources of the self-help niche influences the evolution of the self-help population.

6

Resources: How Competition Selects Only the Fittest Organizations

This chapter examines the same specialty subgroups as the last chapter with respect to their resource use, specifically, the degree to which self-help organizations compete with one another for resources. Unlike public recognition, which depends on cultural alignment between beliefs about acceptable organizational practices and the form these practices take in various types of organizations, competition involves movement organizations vying with one another for the actual resources of their daily activities like members, meeting rooms, and transportation. Likewise, where legitimation indicates differential authority among external actors to permanently shape self-help, the concept of competition highlights the struggle for power over material resources between movement organizations themselves. The two are not unrelated. At the level of individual self-help organizations, legitimation enhances access to resources because legitimate organizations are better able to acquire resources. So, organizations with greater name recognition are likely to be more competitive than those that are unrecognized. Many institutions function in a similar manner. In education, for instance, schools are legitimated by various external sources of authority outside them while they also compete with one another for students, good teachers, and physical resources. Permanence arises through competitive advantage that the most highly recognized enjoy. At the population level, legitimation enhances growth in the size of the movement while competition stabilizes it, by winnowing out less legitimate groups.

Chapter Three detailed the partitioning of self-help resource space by specialty group, using membership as the key to understanding resource use. But membership is not the only resource over which self-help organizations compete: competition also arises for services and social technologies. As discussed throughout this book, social technologies are the means by which groups accomplish their primary goals and can include meetings and discussion groups, psychological peer counseling, visitation programs, and speakers. Self-help services on the other hand can include transportation, study groups, nutritional programs, mother mentoring, special events/social events, educational training, and employment skills. Table 6.1 below summarizes these measures.

It is easy to imagine self-help groups cooperating and sharing resources, which they surely do. Yet, resources are finite and they will ultimately diminish as the population grows larger. A growing population fosters competition between organizations for the materials that help them provide services, maintain their social technologies and membership. This has implications for longevity because organizations that lack access to resources dissolve and the self-help population contracts. Just as the growth of self-help can be explained through examination of the effects of legitimation on organizational formation, the decline of self-help can be assessed by examining the rate at which organizations dissolve. In tandem with the last chapter, three central questions motivate the discussion in this chapter. What are the long-term trends in competition among self-help organizations? How does competition differentially shape the different self-help organizations? And, how does competition differentially affect the dissolution of medical, behavioral, psychological, and general groups? The answers to these questions are straightforward. First, I explore long-term trends in the average amount of resource overlap or competition in services, technologies, and membership and demonstrate that that the general pattern of resource use among self-help groups is remarkably stable over time. While the average amount of resources overall varies slightly, upward and downward trends between resources is apparent. Competition for *members* declines from an initial high during the population's youthful period (1955–1965) and competition for *services* increases, overtaking membership during the mature phase (1985–2000), while *social technologies* hardly changed at all.

Second, I investigate the trajectories competition takes in medical, behavioral, psychological, and general-purpose self-help organizations. In these graphs, I again examine trends over the forty-five-year period in the three types of competition but here I compare services, technologies, and membership for each of the specialty groups. The question is: how does competition vary for each group over time? The analysis shows that not only does the structure of competition change for the different groups, and by whether or not it involves services, technologies, or membership but it varies quite widely between groups over time as well. For example, during self-help's emergent phase psychological groups experience the least amount of competition and general groups the most. By late adolescence, they converge, and then psychological groups experience a much higher average amount of competition than others.

Lastly, I address the issue of the consequences of competition for the dissolution of different groups. Competition influences the extent to which self-help groups survive or not. In short, the ongoing degree of competition between self-help organizations accelerates the decline of the population by driving failure rates higher and higher. To make sense of this relationship, I explore dissolution rates across the different specialty groups for different types of resource overlap. As in the previous chapter, these comparisons are based on simple associations that show the degree to which competition in services, technologies, and membership influences dissolution rates of the different types of self-help organizations. Unlike legitimation, in which some types of legitimation were more important for population viability than others, results show that all three domains of competition, for services, technologies, and membership, have significant effects on subgroup failure. This means that the specialty areas do not monopolize any particular resource but remain competitive among themselves across resource domains.

Table 6.1 Variable Definitions for Dissolution Rates and Competition. National Self-Help/Mutual-Aid Organizations, 1955–2000

Measures	Definitions[a]
Organizational Dissolution Rate	Number of organizations disbanding in a year
Competition	
Services	Transportation, study groups, nutritional programs, mother mentoring, special events/social events, etc.
Social Technologies	Meetings, support, and discussion groups, psychological peer counseling, visitation programs, and speakers etc.
Membership	Patient, family, friends, professionals
Resource Niches	
Medical	Self-help organizations focusing on medical, behavioral, psychological and general conditions
Behavioral	
Psychological	
General-Status	

[a] See Appendix A for a complete listing

How Resources and Competition are Measured

Sources and Types of Self-Help Resources

Self-help organizations use a variety of resources to conduct their daily activities. The *Encyclopedia of Associations* contains information on the types of services, social technologies, and membership for every national self-help group in the movement. Appendix A contains a partial list of the over three hundred services individual self-help organizations offer, and a list of the sixteen different types of social technologies and thirty-four different types of members. Self-help *services* cover a wide range of resources from childcare and libraries to emergency transportation and legal counseling, depending on the specialty niche of the group. Groups compete to have access to resources necessary for the provision of these services. Since services are not generated by the group itself, competition arises when access to the sources of these services such as a local hospital or law firm, or a daycare provider is limited. Self-help *technologies* function in a similar manner. They entail the strategies by which organizational goals are fulfilled. While social technologies may conjure up the image of material resources, they also involve the knowledge and productive activity required to meet organizational ends. As discussed previously, since self-help addresses stigma attached to the illnesses and conditions of its members, their social reintegration is an important organizational end. Self-help technologies consist of the means by which social reintegration is carried out. For example, twelve-step organizations teach the practice of moral principles that are disseminated through support group meetings, visitation programs, and other social technologies (Katz 1993). These principles are conveyed through the particular interactions of the group and serve as a way of life that provide a firm psychological grounding for members as they resume their social roles outside the group. Groups gain a competitive advantage in the arena of social technologies insofar as they offer more meetings than their rivals or provide more flexible visitation schedules and the like.

Self-help *membership* is the third resource over which groups compete. Membership may be limited to those experiencing the problem or stigma defining group membership (e.g., former mental patients, divorcees, the physically handicapped) or it may extend to friends and family (e.g., parents of gays, children of alcoholics). By definition, the groups I have studied in this book are controlled by those who have direct experience with the condition, illness, or problem that identifies the goals of the group (e.g., alcoholism, parents of disabled children, hard of hearing). Individuals may belong to several different types of self-help groups (e.g., Alcoholics Anonymous, Narcotics Anonymous, Al-Anon, CoDA,), and when these overlap in terms of time and interest, competition arises (McPherson 1983).

Competition and Resource Overlap

Competition is a process characterized by resource overlap between individual organizations that is both an individual-level feature of each group as well as an aggregate property of the self-help population. Groups can be characterized by the extent to which they are competitive or not. During the self-help movement's emergence, adolescence and maturity competition arises when self-help organizations overlap in providing access to resources in three areas: services, membership, and technologies. Competition need not be a conscious activity on the part of organizations with respect to other organizations (McPherson 1983). Rather, there is a finite supply of resources, and self-help organizations vie with one another to use them. These organizations may be of the same type or different. For instance, while the Association of Macular Diseases (a self-help group for eye conditions) will not compete with the Allergy Foundation of America (an allergy sufferer's self-help group) in the area of constituency/membership, it still needs to meet in a public space, preferably one with easy access to informational resources, such as a teaching hospital, a facility with special therapeutic equipment, or an outpatient clinic. In this regard, these organizations are in competition with all other "eye/ears/nose and throat" groups dependent on hospitals and clinics for free or inexpensive meeting space. When organizations acquire and extend the same service—such as nutritional programs, childcare, and transportation—resource overlap increases, competition rises, and the pool of resources shrinks. Resources can originate locally or nationally but they exist as a pool that can be tapped only so long as they are available. As resources diminish the number of self-help organizations that depend on them for survival will decline as well.

To the extent that an organization is able to offer unique services, membership, and technologies or to distinguish itself from other similar organizations in the manner of rendered services, membership, and technologies, it will survive relative to those organizations that cannot do so. A number of organizations address various disabilities through self-help support groups. In the 1980s and 1990s, these included the Networking Project for Disabled Women and Girls, Siblings for Significant Change, Siblings of Disabled Children, and American Disability Association, among others. Increase in the services offered by these organizations boosted their chances of increasing membership and other resources important for survival. Both the Networking Project and Siblings of Disabled Children failed to offer the breadth of services the other organizations offered, and therefore disbanded while the others survived.

Constructing a Competition Coefficient

In order to quantify the extent to which one organization may be a successful competitor or not I create a measure of differentiation that reflects the overlap and therefore competition between organizations along the three dimensions of services, social technologies, and membership. This provides individual measures of competitive advantage that can then be averaged for each time period (i.e., 1955, 1956, 1957, and so on until 2000). To arrive at an individual score, differentiation is measured by separating organizations into niche areas based on specialization of function (e.g., marriage and family, infant mortality, cancer, neurological, addiction), and then quantifying differences along the three main dimensions: services (e.g., libraries, computer access, speakers' bureau, publications), social technologies (e.g., meetings, discussion groups, support networks), and membership (e.g., persons with problem or stigma, siblings, family members, partner). To create the coefficient(s), I begin by measuring pairwise overlap among similar types of organizations, and aggregating these pairwise differences across the specialty niche and then for each time period. The formula for calculating the differentiation coefficient is located in an endnote.[1] The main idea is that a score closer to 1 indicates, on average, a greater degree of resource overlap, and lesser differentiation between all organizations in a niche, while a score closer to 0 indicates greater differentiation. To arrive at an average for each time period, the individual scores are added up and divided by the number of existing organizations in the population in each period. The average score for time t, and $t+1$, and $t+2$, and so forth, represents the proportion of groups that overlap on a service, technology, or type of member; in other words, the average amount of competition for the period.

Competition and its Effects

What do I expect regarding long-term trends in competition among self-help organizations? I expect a similar pattern of relationships as found in a variety of populations of organizations such as those in the women's movement, in social services and trade unions, and even among commercial organizations such as breweries. As we saw in Chapter Three, the evolution of these populations is in some ways remarkably similar. It is likely that, initially, competition will be low, given the small number of extant organizations, and as the size of the population grows, competition for the now-diminishing resources of the organizational niche will increase dramatically. Over time, competition will become stronger, organizational dissolution will accelerate relative to organizational foundings, and the size of the population will decline.

Expectations addressing subspecialties are harder to generate in advance because nothing is known about these groups' resource use. It may be that some types of specialties such as medical self-help require more resources than others, but it is equally plausible that there will be little difference between the groups. Similarly, because no studies have explored the dynamics of these organizations, it is impossible to say whether the different dissolution rates will vary between subspecialties, nor can I predict how competition might affect differences in rates. Therefore, the graphs that follow are exploratory in the fullest sense.

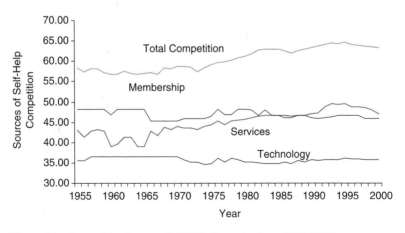

Figure 6.1   Competition between Self-Help Organizations, 1955–2000

I have argued that competition should impact institutionalization of self-help. How does this occur? Competition is a means by which growth in the size of the population is stabilized. Organizations that are redundant with others and those that have failed to attain legitimacy are selected out of the population, that is, they dissolve. Basically, their failure to acquire the resources necessary to survive leads to their dissolution, whether or not they are recognized by legitimating authorities.

Resources and Competition

Services, Technologies and Membership

Patterns that appear in fig. 6.1 depict the unfolding of three types of competition as the self-help population evolves. The upper line shows the combined average for services, social technologies, and membership. There are several points to take away from the graph. First, during population emergence (1955–1970), competition for members is highest, with services and technologies following in decreasing order of importance. The actual numbers can be interpreted as percentages. Nearly 50 percent of all similar self-help organizations compete in terms of the configuration of members who belong to the groups. Over time the average declines enough (to nearly 45 percent during the mature phase—1985–2000) so that competition for services overtakes membership as the greatest source of competition. The extent of competition between organizations in terms of social technologies is almost flat at about 35 percent. Only about a third of self-help organizations at any one time share technologies. This indicates that the mechanisms used by groups to convey their message for engaging in therapeutic support differ across two-thirds of the groups.[2]

The implications are considerable. I anticipated that competition would rise slowly over the evolution of the population, and peak as more and more resources were being used up. Surprisingly, it does not vary greatly but remains relatively stable throughout the forty-five years. The slight upward trend in competition for *services* that parallels the downward trend in competition for *members*, means that beginning around the end of adolescence (1970–1985) and the start of maturity (1985–2000), self-help services are being diminished more than the pool for members. It is difficult to quantify the extent to which the pool is diminished because its limit is an unknown distribution, nor is it clear how many potential constituents or how many potential services there are in the pool and how many organizations can be sustained by it. Instead, it is apparent that there are more members available for self-help than services by the end of the period, such that organizational failure will probably be driven by competition for services and not members. Before addressing this issue, I first examine how trends play out across the four subspecialties. The looming question is: in which areas and between which groups is competition fiercest, and does it remain that way as the population evolves?

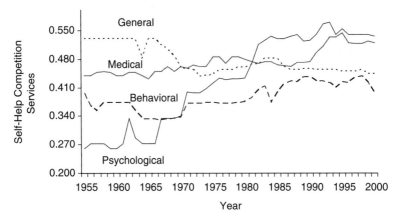

Figure 6.2-A Competition for Services by Self-Help Organizational Subgroup, 1955–2000

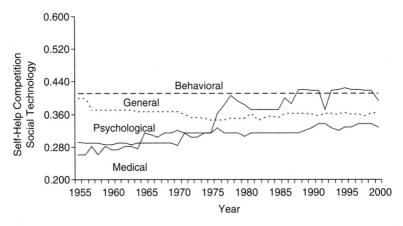

Figure 6.2-B Competition for Social Technology by Self-Help Organizational Subgroup, 1955–2000

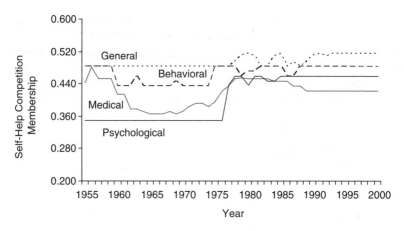

Figure 6.2-C   Competition for Membership by Self-Help Organizational Subgroup, 1955–2000

Competition and Self-Help Subgroups

Just as fig 5.2 described legitimation's relationship with different subspecialties, the graphs in figs. 6.2 depict trends in competition for medical, behavioral, psychological, and general specialty groups. The central question these figures address is: how does competition differentially affect the various self-help organizations? On the basis of the four graphs in total, the answer is that competitive processes operate differentially among the groups. In the last section of this chapter, we will see how differential resource overlap influences the dissolution of these groups in interesting ways. There are a number of important highlights that emerge by comparing the trajectories of the subspecialties. In each graph I begin by comparing trajectories within each source of competition.

During the youthful phase of self-help (1955–1970), competition for services is highest among general-purpose groups (e.g., status groups such as Parents without Partners), followed by medical self-help (e.g., Reach for Recovery), then followed by behavioral groups (e.g., Gamblers Anonymous), and lastly psychological groups (e.g., Depression After Delivery). About half the general-purpose groups overlap on services while only slightly more that a quarter of the psychological groups do. This means that general-purpose groups such as Parents without Partners are much more likely to encroach on one another's services than psychological groups such as Depression After Delivery. Unexpectedly, this changes over time. By late adolescence in the 1980s, psychological groups experienced as much competition as the other groups (almost 50 percent), and by the time the population has become mature, psychological self-help witnesses the highest level of competition (followed by medicine, and then general-purpose groups). Psychological self-help displays the classic pattern of competition for resources: low during the emergent phase, rising steeply during adolescence, then stabilizing through maturity. Both medical and behavioral self-help display an attenuated version of the pattern, while general-purpose, in fact, shows a decline in competition for services over time.

What might be the reason for these trends? It is important first to clarify what it means when competition increases more rapidly for psychological self-help than any other group. It means that it is more likely that the pool of resources for psychology will diminish at a faster rate than for medical, behavioral, and general-purpose self-help. Perhaps fewer of these services exist. As it turns out, the average number of services and the average range of those services is about the same for all of the groups (although behavioral groups have a slightly lower average number of services). Therefore, the types of services are important for the different groups. Again, while medical groups tend to favor a limited number of services, there is nothing to distinguish the other three groups and little to distinguish psychological self-help. The answer is that psychological groups become more alike over time and therefore use more similar resources than the other subspecialties. In fact, three of the four types of specialties are becoming more alike and therefore encroach on each other's resources as time passes. This idea is consistent with the institutionalists' argument that organizations become isomorphic or more alike in order to acquire legitimacy (Scott 2003). Structural similarities between types of organizations leads to greater overlap in resource use.

Comparison of cases underscores this idea. Project Overcome, founded in 1977, is an organization devoted to recovery from mental illness. It secured a niche among mental illness recovery organizations by offering more differentiated recovery services, such as counseling, a speakers' bureau, public education, workshops, advocacy services, consultations, and evaluations, than other mental illness recovery organizations. It scored a .285 on the competition scale. This means that it had a smaller degree of overlap with other organizations (probably because it had quite a number of services). The Living Room, founded in 1959, also focused on recovering mental patients. It scored a .387 on the competition scale. This organization offers only counseling programs but no other unique services, which means that it overlapped many other organizations that also offered counseling programs. Since it did not offer any other unique services, it was in greater competition with a number of other organizations on this dimension.

In the second and third graphs in fig. 6.2, competition for social technologies and membership looks very different than competition for services. Behavioral, followed by general-purpose groups have the highest competition rates for social technologies during the emergence of the population. Next are psychological, then medical groups. While medical groups experience little variation in competition for social technologies, competition between psychological groups begins low (about 28 percent) and then rises sharply during adolescence. Competition for membership, on the other hand, takes a different form. General-purpose groups display the highest level of competition for membership, followed by behavioral and medical groups. Psychological self-help groups display the least amount of membership, competition during the initial stages in the history of the population. Again, psychological self-help jumps up during adolescence and maintains a fairly high level through the mature phase.

That the initial distribution of competition in all these areas varies and then converges during the later years supports the idea that competition increases because of isomorphic tendencies in the population. Recall that measures of competition represent an average or adjusted rate. Changes in the trajectories cannot be due to growth in the population since this factor is considered. Instead, it is likely that as more groups enter the population, they tend to imitate those already there in terms of the structure and purpose of the groups. This in turn translates into similar resource requirements, which increases competition. A good example of two organizations that illustrate this trend is Co-Dependents Anonymous (CoDA) and Adult Children of Alcoholics. Rice (1996) provides an excellent description of the similarities and differences between the groups. The extent to which the two types of organizations are structurally similar, that is, address similar issues through similar mechanisms, is remarkable. Their resource use is also notably similar. While both of these groups survive to this day, declining resources will cause one to become less competitive, leading to its eventual failure. When many of these types of overlaps occur in a subpopulation, dissolution rates will be high, since the resource environment cannot support all organizations seeking the same resources. In the next section, these patterns of relationships suggest that higher dissolution rates occur as a consequence of competition for services, technologies and membership.

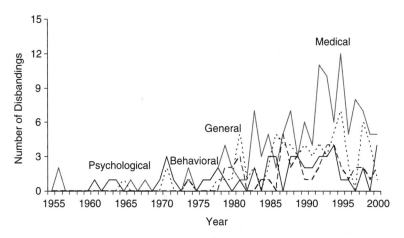

Figure 6.3 Dissolution Rates for Self-Help Organizational Subpopulations, 1955–2000

Competition and Self-Help Rates of Dissolution

Both fig. 6.3 and table 6.2 address dissolution of self-help organizations for the different subspecialties. Before we explore these trends, recall from Chapter Three that organizational dissolution rates are counts of the number of organizations that disband during any one of the forty-five years of the population's existence.[3] In fig. 6.3, the dissolution rates display a notable pattern: despite some spiking, the trend is toward fairly low rates of dissolution from the emergence of the population through adolescence. Rates seem to be about the same for all groups, hovering under five dissolutions every couple of years. Around the early 1980s general-purpose groups and medical groups begin to experience accelerated failure. Medical organizations continue a steep failure rate until the mid-1990s, when their dissolution starts to relax. Psychological groups dissolve at a low rate, which is indicated by the flat line.

How does competition differentially affect the dissolution of medical, behavioral, psychological, and general groups? The effect of resource use on failure rates indicates whether competition causes self-help groups to fail. This is important since it is often presumed that movement organizations engage in cooperative rather than competitive relations with one another (Katz 1993). The real question is whether the notion of cooperation is about activists' goodwill rather than the actual sharing of resources.

Table 6.2 Coefficients Measuring the Strength of Association between Competition and Dissolution Rates

Sources of Competition	Medical Dissolution Rate[a]	Behavioral Dissolution Rate	Psychological Dissolution Rate	General Dissolution Rate
Services	0.727*	0.613*	0.580*	−0.491*
Social Technologies	0.583*	−0.141	0.500*	−0.244
Membership	0.293*	0.347*	0.516*	0.673*

[a] Starred * numbers indicate .05 level of significance or less

The previous figures show that different competitive processes operate in different self-help groups. This final section addresses the question of the extent to which differential competition affects the dissolution of medical, behavioral, psychological, and general self-help. As in the previous chapter, one way to quantify the influence of competition on organizational dissolution is to look at a measure of association that captures how strongly competition matches the dissolution rates for the different groups. Table 6.2 contains these correlations. As discussed above, organizational ecology predicts that as competition rises, so too will the rate at which self-help organizations dissolve. To make the link more plausible, I lag competition a year before dissolution. In other words, competition is measured prior to the dissolution rate so as to eliminate the possibility that increases in dissolution can influence the degree to which organizations are competing. Naturally, there will be other factors that influence the rate at which self-help organizations dissolve. For instance, voluntary organizations such as self-help depend on members to sustain the organization. The simplest explanation for failure among voluntary associations is an individual-level explanation: members exit, which leads to a decline in commitment and participation resulting in organizational disbanding. In general terms this thesis is always true: organizations need members to sustain them. How much membership loss can an organization sustain and still survive? The answer is not known in this case. Toughlove International, Alcoholic Anonymous, and Al-Anon all experienced membership loss during the 1990s without dissolving. With no systematic measures of membership patterns, competition serves as a reasonable way to understand how differences in resources influence the survival of the four specialties.

Based on criteria elaborated in table 5.2, some cutoff values will help make sense of the relationship between competition and the four types of groups. As mentioned, any correlation from .10 through .30 indicates a small but meaningful relationship, and .30 through .50 is a moderate-sized one. Correlations above .50 are strong. Also, correlations that are starred indicate that the relationship is significantly different from 0 (at the .05 level or less of significance) to warrant our attention.

Dissolution rates, as we had thought, are a function of competition among self-help organizations for services, social technologies, and members. The pattern of relationships is compelling. Increases in competition for services, social technologies, and members result in medical and psychological self-help dissolution. Unexpectedly, social technologies are *not* related to behavioral and general dissolution, and, competition for services is negatively related to the dissolution of general-purpose groups. In effect, declining competition for services is related to increases in general-purpose dissolution. Yet, the latter might not be so very odd, given that general-purpose self-help witnessed this peculiar dynamic: resource overlap decreased rather than increased as the population aged. Therefore, its rising dissolution rate (fig. 6.3) was met with a falling competition rate that stabilized soon after it began to fall. While medical dissolution is consistently related to increases in the average level of competition for services and social technologies, its relationship with membership is small, relative to the other two coefficients. Similarly, dissolution of psychological groups is also related to these three factors, but competition for membership retains a fairly strong relationship with the dissolution of psychological groups. Naturally, I would need to include other factors in the model to make a stronger case for these influences, but the two are clearly related.

Based on the size of the coefficients, membership seems to be important for psychological and general-purpose self-help, but less so for medical and behavioral rates. In general, competition for services leads to consistent declines, and overlap in social technologies does as well. Trends suggest that competition translates into a greater likelihood of the dissolution of self-help groups, but it sometimes depends on the type of competition. This is the story that the pattern of relationships in this table reveals.

Competition for resources among self-help organizations is contingent on the specialty niche and the evolution of the population. While competition among self-help groups overall does not rise and peak in the way it might in commercial or bureaucratic populations, it does so for some organizational subgroups. Overlap among psychological organizations remained low during the emergent phases of the movement and then rose steadily until competition among groups for services and membership peaked. Other types of organizations witnessed changes in their competitive niches, but these were minor compared to psychological groups. Interestingly, intense competition among psychological groups did not result in their having higher than usual rates of dissolution. That distinction was captured by medical self-help.

Self-help organizations attempt to manage crowding in markets by targeting unique resource segments in an effort to reduce competition when different organizations converge on a single resource or production space (Carroll and Hannan, 2000). By differentiating themselves from potential competitors along a number of formal dimensions, organizations that do not enjoy scale advantages (e.g., usually newer or smaller organizations) can exploit variations in available resource space even when a market has attained a high degree of concentration. Using a resource-based framework to detail the relationship between the formal aspects of organizations such as their subspecialty and the trajectory of growth and decline helps us understand the mechanisms underlying these dynamics. Yet, given that organizations confront both institutional and competitive pressures, how are researchers to understand the cross-cutting mechanisms generating organizational legitimation and viability, and, competition? What can organizations do to foster legitimation, promote viability, and assure persistence, when all along, competitive pressures continually threaten? One way to understand this tension is that all organizations get public recognition by imitating other similar organizations (Scott 2003). This process generates population-level homogeneity, generates more examples of the form, and reduces disbanding. To the extent that an organizational population is homogenous, we might expect an exponential rise in competition (since every organization is competing with every other one for the same resources). The dilemma seems profound and organizations theorists have struggled to understand the tension for decades. Practically, to the extent that competition refines the pool of organizations in the movement, winnowing out less legitimate ones, it may increase the taken-for-grantedness of those that remain.

7

Conclusion and Future Directions

The Evolution of Self-Help

Self-help is now taken for granted in the United States. Its presence can be observed in bookstores and libraries, which contain shelves of material devoted to every form imaginable. Moreover, popular media reference self-help as a literary genre or as a psychotherapeutic group phenomenon, without resorting to long explanations about what is meant. These references usually consist of a group of men and women seated on folding chairs in a circle in some rented meeting space, coffee cups in hand, sharing the intimate experience of their debilitating condition, or that of a relative or loved one. The evocation of this scene from the *Simpsons* and *Sopranos* to James Frey's addiction memoir featured on Oprah's book-of-the-month club signals the ubiquity and taken-for-grantedness of self-help. As I have argued, self-help support groups have emerged as *the way* of solving a number of medical, behavioral, and psychological problems. However, how and why this took place in mid-century American culture remains a question that despite several decades' worth of research is still largely open to speculation. Indeed, while an extensive body of theoretical and empirical research details the reasons people join groups, their dynamics, and relations with professionals, less is known about the growth, decline, and persistence of the population of organizations called self-help, or about the social, cultural, and political forces shaping it than might be expected given the prevalence of the phenomenon. Certainly a good thirty years' worth of scholarly and popular studies have contributed greatly to our knowledge of key aspects of the self-help phenomenon. And yet, despite research covering the self-help movement and its ideological underpinnings, the question about how this health movement became institutionalized—the diffusion of the form, its social, political, and popular legitimation and its competitive fitness—has not been explored at length. In fact, given self-help's presence in the culture at large, more needs to be said about how and why it got that way. For example, while self-help advocates were promoting the rise and ubiquity of self-help support groups and marveling that there was a self-help group for every class of disorder identified by the World Health Organization during the late 1980s and 1990s (Kurtz 1997), the empirical fact was that founding rates of self-help were declining and dissolution rates were climbing (Chapter Three). It is interesting that most organizational populations, from newspapers to social service agencies, show the same trajectories. This suggests that the dynamics shaping institutionalization of self-help are similar to those influencing other very different organizational forms. At the same time, analyses in this book also describe how different self-help is from other organizational forms on a number of dimensions.

One of the chief problems in undertaking the task of explaining what processes led to the growth and permanence of self-help is to delineate which social processes lend themselves to institutionalization in the first place. Some self-help scholars regard self-help from the point of view of the broader culture. McGee's (2005) recent work details the relationship between self-help and American's longstanding penchant for self reinvention while Rice (1996) emphasizes the widespread cultural acceptance of psychotherapy as a precursor of self-help. Similarly, Hurvitz (1976) claims self-help is an outcome of the convergence of psychotherapeutic and religious traditions in American culture. In most of these accounts, self-sufficiency and self-mastery are the themes linking self-help with other prominent American institutions. The underlying assumption is that modern self-help proposes to teach people skills to evaluate their own psyches. For purposes of self-mastery, the solution to problems of cancer and mental illness and addiction is offered by different groups in the form of a reinvented self, such as cancer survivor, or recovering addict. These various cultural explanations of self-help explain how societal-level symbolic categories undergird its widespread acceptance. The process is a top-down one in which practices get encoded in new organizational forms such as self-help support groups and spread in such a way that leads to their eventually becoming taken for granted. I have referred to this process as enactment because symbolic categories like the reinvented self become the script for how self-help organizations do what they do.

This book modifies this cultural approach by taking a slightly more structural view. It argues for the importance of seeing self-help in organizational terms, as a health social movement. In this framework, the origins and ultimate acceptance of self-help is not a function of cultural elements alone, which filter down to the local level, but of structural forces that create opportunities for diffusion of organizational practices from the bottom up. These foster local problem-solving efforts that diffuse across the movement in the form of individual albeit similar organizational forms. Self-help is a challenger movement, forged in opposition to institutionalized healthcare. Its organizations, although largely unallied, advocate for change in the healthcare sector by opposing mainstream healthcare authority, formulating new policy, and altering legal systems. Like other movements, self-help activists mobilize constituents to garner funds for research, challenge regulations and laws, and foster public discussion about the social conditions underlying their problems. Self-help differs from other social movements, and from some health movements in that its members seek change at the individual level first, rather than in the political system (although the latter may follow from support group participation). This focus on personal experience and transformation is consistent with the diverse components of the field of self-help that range from ideologies and programs to support groups. I argued that self-help constitutes a health social movement because it strives for formal and informal change in healthcare systems, and challenges institutional authority, broadly construed. Self-help provides a well-known set of alternative beliefs and practices, and fosters a new social identity linked to membership in the movement. Although many self-help organizations deal with physical disability and illness, we call self-help a *health* movement not because of its members' focal condition. It would not be completely accurate to do so since there are self-help groups dealing with status issues that do not seem to address health per se. Rather, it is the social technology of self-help, its psychosocial support groups, oriented toward restoring psychological well-being, through therapeutic conversation, that constitutes the definition of self-help as a health movement.

In the tradition of American self-sufficiency anyone can organize a psychotherapeutic support group to counsel the stigmatized, provide services, and extend the delivery of healthcare, if not actually help reformulate health policy by taking advantage of political alliances. If self-reinvention is a quintessential American characteristic (McGee 2005) then one of the most interesting questions about how Americans reinvent themselves is to ask about the culturally unique ways they go about doing so. As noted elsewhere, this do-it-yourself method of healthcare has a particular cultural resonance consistent with a socio-political history of self-sufficiency (often accompanied by isolation-ism) as well as an ideology of mutual assistance. Self-help organizations are the material instances of broad cultural scripts that prize individ-ual motivation and rational action. They are the organizational solu-tion to the problem of getting collective/public action out of individual/ private problems. De Tocqueville and others have remarked on this behavior with regard to the temperance movement of the mid-nine-teenth century, a peculiarly American affair, but also one which, some have argued (Young 2002), contributed to the rise of national social movements in the United States (cf. Tilly 2002). Not surprisingly, slightly more than a century later, self-help arose under similar condi-tions—a burgeoning women's movement, religious revivalism, tem-perance, and radical changes in mainstream medicine. The later period was also a time when the U.S. social movement sector became steeped in identity politics. As in other movements beginning in the 1960s, self-help organizational goals included identity reconstruction based on homogenous group membership in which socially embattled and stigmatized identities were converted into socially acceptable (even idealized) ones. This may, in part, be due to the odd cultural convergence of liberal self-help and conservative Christian and Jewish traditions in the United States—those who embraced the stigmatized identity (or a sinful one, as these religious traditions would have it) experienced more successful group integration as a testament to the legitimacy and power of the group's mission.

For self-help, reconstructing the identity of individuals and bringing about public reintegration paralleled the diffusion of its organiza-tional practices.[1] The proliferation of its support groups was the way in which reconstituted identities took collective form and through which self-help had its most profound impact on American culture. Some researchers see organizations as the locus of institutionalization and others see institutionalization processes occurring at the societal level. Sometimes social movements are involved and other times the carriers of institutions are state actors and professions. Naturally there are a number of mechanisms by which self-help became what it is today. These are described in broad strokes in the self-help litera-ture. My main focus, however, has been to empirically analyze the diffusion of self-help practices at the formal level. In short, the central question is: how do marginalized practices, particularly healthcare practices dominated by medical professionals, become mainstream (Ruggie 2004)? The answer in this book, as depicted in the graphs and tables, and told through organizational histories, is that legitimacy and competition shape self-help's role vis-à-vis mainstream healthcare.

Among self-help actors, diffusion occurs as independent organizational forms are created to meet healthcare needs that established medicine and social welfare services fail to adequately provide. Later, groups adopt similar forms and practices to solve problems of unmet needs that might have been solved through other designs but mimic a particular organization because of its legitimacy. The example I gave compared the early founders of addiction-related self-help groups (e.g., Alcoholics Anonymous, Al-Anon, Addicts Anonymous) with later anonymous organizations (e.g., Gamblers Anonymous and Emotions Anonymous). The anonymous twelve-step organizational form became the legitimate template for many conditions other than that for which it was originally designed. The key mechanism by which this occurs is that as the number of adopters increases, relevant authorities endorse their innovation, which gains legitimacy and becomes the norm. Although it might sound counterintuitive, physicians and other medical professionals who supported the development of alternative practices such as self-help are central to institutionalization. It would seem that alternative practices are likely to lead to fragmentation and disruption of medical hegemony over healthcare, so why would professionals help in the diffusion of a set of contested beliefs and practices? As I argued, self-help organizers were able to finesse the acquisition of legitimacy by coopting select professionals who supported the goals of self-help. Political and academic actors had greater influence on founding rates than medical professionals.

How did this occur? At the broadest level of sociopolitical opportunity, the state indirectly shaped the growth of self-help through its role as the largest purchaser of healthcare in the 1960s, which led to the fragmentation of medical professional hegemony (Scott et al. 2000) and opened the field to complementary and alternative practices. State deregulation of healthcare and the emergence of market logics in the 1980s led to even more splintering of professional dominance and the burgeoning of self-help. Self-help organizers were active at this time in framing alternative healthcare practices as a preeminent method of prevention that may have appealed to some types of practitioners, especially those just entering the field. For instance, the rise of the treatment industry in the late 1970s and early 1980s, fueled by third-party payments, brought physicians and healthcare professionals into more intimate contact with recovering members of self-help groups, who then contributed to growth in the industry by seeking work at the very places where they had been "rehabilitated" (White 1998). These actors imported their self-help practices into more formalized settings. In this case, the spread of beliefs and practices among local actors became instrumental in shaping changes in established healthcare practices.

Although it is seductive to portray the emergence of self-help largely on the basis of universal themes like individualism, or else as a consequence of unmet needs resulting in diffusion of organizations to solve those problems, the growth of self-help is a multilevel process that also entails sociopolitical conflict, negotiation, and resolution. Importantly, as a challenger to institutionalized healthcare, self-help faces a number of problems in the process of diffusion that mainstream actors engaged in conventional political contests do not. That is, in addition to winning over professionals, how do challenger organizations acquire the necessary legitimacy from institutional sources when these sources represent their antagonists? In a very important sense, as much as self-help represents a legitimated, newly institutionalized set of beliefs and practices, it occupies a radical position vis-à-vis mainstream healthcare (see Ruggie 2004).

Using an organizations-social movement schema, we saw how enactment, diffusion, and politics foster the conditions under which self-help emerged and led to the institutionalization of the movement. Each emphasizes one aspect of the process. The ideological case provides the cultural context, the social-structural case emphasizes diffusion of practices based on unmet needs, and the political one helps us understand the role that political struggles take in shaping the evolution of self-help. But because there was no systematic link between the movement and its organizations in previous research, the way in which ideology, diffusion, and politics combine to foster the self-help movement, its trajectory and ultimate persistence was an empirical mystery.

Borrowing this schema helps frame the basic demographic processes described in the empirical chapters. What is necessary to analyze the various claims related to this schema is to examine the patterns of organizational formation and dissolution, legitimation and competition, and resource use for the population as a whole. Lacking self-help demographic data, no research addressed the basic issue of how self-help organizational forms are reproduced and evolve over time, and none offered very comprehensive descriptions of the processes by which the self-help organizational form became institutionalized. For example, are some authorities more important for the emergence or for the dissolution of self-help organizations and how? What resources are necessary for the persistence of self-help? To answer these and other questions, we needed a dataset that had information on self-help organizations over the course of major growth from the 1950s through the end of the century. Chapter Three detailed the elements of the dataset and protocol under which it was created. By creating a dataset that contains information about self-help organizations, I am able to address these questions and to understand how marginal practices become more mainstream. In the empirical chapters I began by showing the growth and diversification of these organizations as they captured different healthcare markets. To the extent that self-help captures different markets for their services, legitimation of the form grows as well. This is not simply a speculative observation. With this dataset I could actually show how legitimation of the form diffuses (in Chapter Five). While the empirical emphasis is on diffusion, political contention driven by social movement actors who borrow from a wealth of symbolic cultural elements forms the mechanism for the legitimation of self-help and its growth.

Empirical Findings

I began with a number of key questions related to the institutionalization of self-help by developing a systematic survey of the growth, decline, and persistence of self-help organizations. The overarching question was: Do the same conditions that generate resource partitioning in commercial sectors promote the phenomenon in the alternative healthcare sector, at least with respect to this population of organizations? Answering this question lays the groundwork for understanding how organizational populations vie for resources and how resource partitioning takes place generally across a number of populations.

Interestingly, the growth, decline, and persistence of self-help resembles the dynamics and diversification of a variety of commercial and noncommercial organizational populations. In these populations, founding rates decline because crowding in organizational populations limits access to resources for new organizations (e.g., see Carroll and Hannan 2000). However, in mature populations, a few large organizations eventually come to dominate a sector or market, and new organizations spring up to take advantage of specialty niches that remain open (Carroll 1985). It is compelling to ask whether this theory, which has been examined for commercial organizations, also predicts similar developments among self-help. That is, does the emergence of large dominant *subpopulations* of self-help organizations limit access to resources by other organizations? The answer was unexpected: while the self-help market overall is dominated by specialists (in contrast to expectations of resource partitioning), the main historical trend is away from increasing specialization and generalist concentration, and toward greater generalism among all organizations. There is a strong tendency toward *less* concentration in both social welfare and medical subpopulations, as well as less concentration within specialist populations and (surprisingly) generalist populations. As I noted earlier, this has several implications. It might mean that the population is not mature enough to display the same resource partitioning trends as other populations or that the underlying processes are very different from those found in commercial sectors. Note however that it is strikingly similar to other populations in its basic trajectory. Thus, the differences are probably real, suggesting that the underlying processes differ. That the underlying causes are different is informative and compelling. Substantively, there appears to be growing involvement of outsiders in self-help organizations. This is not unexpected. Since the focus of the study is national self-help organizations, they likely became national by allying themselves with professional authorities outside of the movement.

The next step was to describe the particular socioeconomic, political, and organizational features of these population environments in order to answer the question why the distribution shifts in this particular way (e.g., perhaps due to legitimacy). I explored two important aspects of this question in the chapters that followed by examining the processes by which self-help gains legitimation and uses material resources. The two central questions that motivated the discussion of this issue were: how do self-help organizations acquire legitimacy to promote their causes, and, which sources are most important for recognition?

Chapter Four took up the issue of legitimation. It showed the tenuousness of legitimation processes that challenger organizations experience by analyzing medical, academic, popular, and political types and sources of legitimation that underlie the self-help movement. The effectiveness of voluntary organizations, such as self-help, is judged in terms of "social criteria like the satisfaction and approval of external constituencies" (Singh et al. 1991:392). So, the nature of these external constituencies becomes pressing, especially when actors confront conflicting normative requirements generated by different authorities. This motivated the central questions of the chapter: how and where do oppositional enterprises gain legitimacy? I addressed these questions with exploration of the tensions that challenger organizations experience as a result of the necessity of seeking legitimation from established authorities. One way self-help organizations acquire legitimacy is through organizers such as Abraham Low, Bill Wilson, Jolly K., Dr. Greg Meissen, professor of psychology at Wichita State University, and former Surgeon General Everett Koop who serve as bridges between the domains. Social movement organizers are essential in the transformation of familiar organizational models for new purposes, and extend accompanying legitimation frames attached to those established forms.

Examination of the organizational histories of self-help reveals that all of them attempt to gain recognition by highlighting political appearances, academic seminars, popular talks and speeches, and other special events that link the organization to important external authorities. I described this process in the discussion of Parents Anonymous, the National SIDS Foundation, and the National Alliance for the Mentally Ill. In these cases, legitimation emerged from media, professional, and political authority. For Parents Anonymous, radiologists' and pediatricians' involvement in child abuse discovery explicitly framed the nature of the trauma in medico-scientific terms, so that any reasonable individual would be certain of its authenticity. Since claims made by medical doctors about health issues are putatively more influential than laypersons' explanatory schemes, organizers who have medical degrees are better placed to legitimate self-help. In the case of the National SIDS Foundation, Bergman's presidency of the organization established its reputation as a political organization as well as a support group. The National SIDS Foundation's access to political resources was considerable. In the case of NAMI, political activism garnered federal monies while popular recognition in *Women's Day* and the *New Yorker* generated sympathy and acceptance. For NAMI, connection to the medical community takes the form of psychiatrists who sit on its advisory council. For these organizations, attachment to institutional actors (such as a medical school or psychology department) is likely to enhance the degree to which an organization is seen as appropriate and intelligible, and deserving of recognition. This in turn makes forming other similar organizations feasible, promotes organizational viability, and contributes in the aggregate to expansion of the movement.

Legitimation processes are dependent on key entrepreneurial activities that accumulate over time in a series of occasions for recognition. Interestingly, while seeking institutional support, self-help maintains a fairly radical stance with respect to mainstream healthcare, asserting that professionals have "monopolize[d] definitions, diagnosis and treatment of problems people face" and neglected "their clients' self-understanding, self-management and self-reliance," resulting in clients' increased "dependency and passivity" (Katz 1993:71). This exacerbates conditions under which organizers' intervention becomes crucial because wholesale rejection of self-help by mainstream institutional authorities who do not believe they monopolize definitions nor neglect their patients would seem a natural reaction. Since all social movements pass through periods of varying support and hostility (McAdam, Tarrow, and Tilly 2001), it is important to delineate the specific conditions and practices that facilitate bridging between the movement and various institutional domains so that the processes by which institutionalization occurs become clearer. In Chapter Four, I was able to identify several sources of legitimation that bridge social movement and institutional domains in the complementary and alternative healthcare sector. Still, by focusing on only four instances of legitimation, it is impossible to know how it develops as the movement ages. Are some sources of legitimation more important than others and how do these influence the institutionalization of self-help? To answer these questions I explored the broader consequences of public recognition as a series of trends in legitimation rates in the following chapter.

In the longitudinal analyses taken up in Chapter Five, the goal was to explain how temporal processes foster the growth of legitimation of self-help. While case studies show how activists work to establish connections between self-help and mainstream healthcare, investigation of longitudinal rates shows how different types of legitimation at the population level unfold over the evolution of the movement. Another way of thinking about these analyses is in terms of the diffusion of practices that are in the process of being institutionalized. Legitimation of self-help practices by medical, academic, popular, and political audiences is the mechanism by which institutionalization takes place. The three research questions that motivated the discussion were: 1) are some sources of legitimation more important than others; 2) do these have differential effects on different types of self-help organizations—how long do they last, and; 3) how does differential recognition affect their formation? We learned, in short, that different sources of public recognition vary in the attention paid to self-help. We saw that attention varied dramatically both between the different sources, and over the course of the forty-five years. I compared the sources of legitimation for each of the specialty groups. Findings indicated that not only are different kinds of authority important for different kinds of groups but these influences vary over time as well. For example, surprisingly, political recognition was more important than medical, academic, and popular recognition for medical self-help groups such as Mended Hearts and Epilepsy Concern. In contrast, academic recognition was more important than the others for behavioral self-help groups such as Gamblers Anonymous. What accounts for this pattern is that political alliances are more likely to be sought by medical groups, all else being equal, whose members' status (such as Dr. Abraham for NSIDSF) assure greater access. Here the similarities between political movements and self-help may be the greatest.

Lastly, I addressed the consequences of public recognition for the viability of self-help organizations, since institutionalization follows from organizational growth and legitimation. Although legitimation at the organizational level may be worth obtaining, public recognition has consequences for the evolution of the population: it influences the extent to which self-help groups are formed and the population grows. Without a legitimate organizing template, founders pursue other means of setting up their groups. This process has a critical point where the degree of recognition suddenly accelerates the growth of the self-help population and fosters dramatic increases in group formation. To make sense of this trend, I examined the founding rates for the different specialty groups and compared these rates across the various sources of legitimation. These comparisons were based on simple measures of association that show the degree to which public recognition in one domain, for example, popular legitimation, influences the founding rates of different self-help organizations. In contrast to the individual influence of medical legitimation, findings indicated that recognition of medical authorities barely mattered when it came to founding new self-help organizations in any of the four niches. On the other hand, the extent to which groups in certain niches acquired political capital had an important effect on the likelihood of organizations forming in that niche. As noted, medical self-help is indebted to political authorities for recognition and this recognition translates into higher founding rates. In contrast, behavioral groups such as Gamblers Anonymous and Al-Anon find legitimation in academic circles, rather than in political communities. Finally, that popular legitimation served to promote self-help formation, but only for groups occupying the medical and behavioral niches, begs the question as to why for these niches and not the other two? In fact, the negative coefficients indicate that recognition had a detrimental effect on founding rates. One reason may be that these niches became so crowded over time that organizers who might otherwise have been tempted to form new groups in these areas decided not to do so because of lack of resources in that particular niche. For psychological self-help this is probably the case since, as we saw in the final chapter, competitive overlap in all resource areas was most dramatic for these organizations (see figs. 6.2). But this explanation does not account for organizations providing resources around general psychological problems, those primarily associated with status and legal issues. These groups expanded threefold between 1955 and 2000 (see table 3.1). Again, control over resources may be the underlying explanation for the negative effect of popular recognition on founding rates of status support groups. We might conclude then that legitimating authority is not a single generic entity but a varied set of rules and practices governing recognition of self-help groups, and these are conditioned by the different markets into which self-help ventures. To make this explicit, the final empirical chapter explored the effects of resource use and competition within and across the four markets in the self-help population.

In that chapter, I examined the same subgroups with respect to their resource use, specifically, the degree to which self-help organizations compete with one another for resources. Competition involves organizational struggles over material bases of survival. Legitimation and competition are intertwined in these conflicts. For individual self-help organizations legitimation enhances access to resources and reduces costs so that those with greater name recognition are likely to be more competitive than those that go unrecognized. Many institutions function in a similar manner. Healthcare organizations are legitimated by various external sources of authority while they also compete with one another for patients, physicians and administrators, and physical resources. Permanence arises through competitive advantage that the most highly recognized enjoy. At the population level, legitimation enhances growth in the size of the movement while competition stabilizes it by winnowing out less legitimate groups.

First, I explored long-term trends in the average amount of resource overlap or competition in services, technologies, and membership and learned that the general pattern of resource use among self-help groups is remarkably stable over time. Competition for *members* declined from an initial high during the population's youthful period (1955–1965) and competition for *services* increased, overtaking membership during the mature phase (1985–2000), while *social technologies* hardly changed at all. Next I addressed the question: How does competition differentially affect various types of self-help organizations? As we saw with respect to legitimation, the answer is that competitive processes operate differently among the groups. Competition for services was highest among status groups (about half the general-purpose groups overlap on services), followed by medical, behavioral, and then psychological groups. However, by late adolescence in the 1980s, psychological groups experienced as much competition as the other groups (almost 50 percent), and then in maturity, psychological self-help witnessed the most competition of all (followed by medicine, and then general-purpose groups).

How did varying competition affect the dissolution of medical, behavioral, psychological, and general groups? Increases in competition for services, social technologies, and members, in the case of medical and psychological groups, resulted in medical and psychological self-help dissolution. What I did not expect was that social technologies were unrelated to behavioral and general dissolution, and, competition for services was negatively related to the dissolution of general-purpose groups. Membership seems to be important for psychological and general-purpose self-help, but less so for medical and behavioral rates. In all, self-help organizations attempt to manage crowding in markets by targeting unique resource segments in an effort to reduce competition when different organizations converge on a single resource. This exercise in explaining competitive overlap in self-help organization helps us understand the processes of resource distribution in organizational populations more broadly, since competition does vary by market niche for diverse organizational populations (Carroll 1985).

Contributions and Implications

This study advances understanding of self-help and health social movements in several ways. First, this research answers some basic demographic questions about the growth of self-help that have not been systematically addressed (Chapter Three): what are the varieties of national self-help organizations, when did they arise, how do they grow, do they decline and by how much, what kinds of resource niches do they capture, which ones predominate and what happens when certain types of organizations monopolize the population? Answering these questions highlights the differences and similarities between commercial and noncommercial organizational populations. The result is that at least with regard to its trajectory of growth and stabilization, self-help resembles many other populations of organizations. In the manner of its resource partitioning, self-help differs dramatically. The question, though, is whether the mechanisms by which these basic patterns emerge are similar or different. One way to address this question is by making assumptions about self-help's categorical status: is it more or less like other healthcare movement organizations? The answer is that it resembles other movements that emphasize members' illness experiences as a source of sociopolitical and cultural change and therefore the underlying processes driving their growth and persistence are probably similar to those health movement organizations.

This draws us into the social movement literature. Following Snow (2004), Cress and Myers (2004), and others (Cohen and Arato 1992), I view social movements as contention between groups of challengers and institutionalized authority, broadly construed. Contention includes but is not limited to political struggles between social movement actors and the state, as the most powerful constituted authority. Self-help contests medical and scientific practice and knowledge through struggles with medical professionals, scientific research, media, and industry. This means that self-help organizations can be seen as movement-like by virtue of their implicit and explicit struggle with professional, political, and popular antagonists. Moreover, self-help has influenced public attitudes and policy regarding mutual aid, social support, the nature of recovery, and other issues (Katz 1993).

By extending this theoretical framework, the second contribution this study makes is that it supplements a growing list of research studies that examine organizational challenges to authority outside of the domain of the state (see Snow's 2004). Interestingly, a few of these studies look specifically at self-help groups (e.g., Taylor 1996 and Rice 1996), although none adopt the organizations-social movement perspectives used here. Health social movements have become important vehicles for integrating social movement and organizations perspectives because the healthcare literature describes radical institutional change in need of the kind of explanations that these two perspectives offer (Brown et al. 2004; Brown and Zavestoski 2004; Zavestoski et al. 2004). This study develops these explanations by linking legitimation, competition, and self-help viability. Analyzing self-help within this framework allows us to understand how self-help members, activists, and entrepreneurs strategize to deal with multiple authorities with varying agendas and resources. In analyses in Chapters Four and Five, I was able not only to identify authorities (professional and political alliances) relevant to self-help growth but to analyze which ones are the most important. Professional and political alliances foster legitimation by demonstrating to interested constituencies the sociopolitical connections between collective actors. Although I do not explore the implications of these strategic alliances and political connections for sociopolitical opportunities giving rise to self-help in this book, these data can be used to address issues related to sociopolitical opportunities.

As this study and others (e.g., Sandell 2001) have shown, the expansion of organizational populations virtually takes on a life of its own. Social processes like legitimation (and competition), once set in motion, have persistent effects that result in new configurations of organizations. Study of the rise of a population of organizations, such as self-help, particularly through analysis of organizational (ecological and institutional) variation, provides insight into legitimation and competitive processes that analysis of a single organization does not.

The results of empirical analysis supported several ideas and suggested the effectiveness of their application beyond their original research. Using a resource-based framework to detail the relationship between the formal aspects of organizations helps us understand the competitive mechanisms underlying institutionalization. To the extent that organizations capture different markets for their services, legitimation of the form diffuses as well. This is not simply a speculative observation but one confirmed by the empirical work in this book.

Yet, given that organizations confront both institutional and competitive pressures, how are researchers to understand the cross-cutting mechanisms generating organizational legitimation, competition, and viability? What can organizations do to promote viability, and assure persistence, when all along, competitive pressures continually threaten? To the extent that an organizational form becomes structurally embedded in a sector, its taken-for-grantedness guarantees its fitness even in the face of competitive pressures (DiMaggio and Powell 1991).

How this comes about is that the struggle for legitimation is situated in a larger sociopolitical context.

Consequently, I add a social movement framework here to the organizations one in order to help us understand contention between mainstream and alternative actors over what constitutes appropriate healthcare practices. Health social movements challenge prevailing social and cultural institutional orders (Brown et al. 2004). They attempt to alter not only societal-level political institutions but authority structures that operate at multiple social system levels, whether in public, private, or semi-private arenas of politics, commerce, and social life generally (Fligstein 1998; Gamson and Meyer 1996). Just as self-help challenges medical authority while trying to win over healthcare professionals, studies of health consumer movements (Allsop, Jones, and Baggott 2004), abortion rights campaigns (Joffe, Weitz, and Stacey 2004) and breast cancer (Klawiter 2004) show how these challengers target not only policymakers but professional bodies, corporations, countermovements, and public opinion in an effort to bring about institutional change. Focusing only on direct challenges to the polity limits investigating the full range of (political and cultural) contexts within which struggles with authority take place. By studying only political movements and the state, we miss the generality of social movement-like processes that characterize life in a number of sectors such as healthcare. Emphasizing challenges in multiple domains expands the analytic horizon beyond episodes of social movement and state confrontation, and permits greater differentiation of potential influence of actors operating in sociopolitical, economic, and cultural environments. The solution adopted in this book was to theorize self-help in health movement and organizational terms based on the actual sociopolitical authority structures it confronts, such as medical professionals, so that lessons learned about, for instance, the salutary influence of political legitimation for medical self-help, or the corrosive effects of competition for services, among medical, behavioral, and psychological groups, can then be extended to our understanding of consumer, abortion, and cancer movements (among others).

This flexible framework provides an important theoretical tool for the task of explaining the growth of self-help because it describes the interaction of organizational and institutional forces. It is therefore likely that for other movements, legitimation and competition are vital in formation and disbanding. This general dynamic highlights the processes by which these organizations create an independent niche in the alternative healthcare sector (Maton 1989).

Caveats

The first limitation of this study is linked to its strength: demographic questions about the growth of self-help. By collapsing the field into a population of national self-help organizations, it assumes that organizations and their members are all alike. Yet, there is a remarkable diversity of actors, interests, and practices in self-help that remain unanalyzed when composite data such as these are used. For example, I do not take up the question of the underlying motivations of individual participation and mobilization of individuals. Based on a number of excellent studies, I assume that individuals form groups to address a range of problems for the same reasons and with the same degree of commitment that they organize around political concerns. This is not to say that all self-help groups are the same. It simply suggests that knowing individuals' motivations for joining groups will not help us map out the trajectory by which self-help becomes institutionalized. Motivations are always tricky. Do motivations matter when extending an organizations-social movement framework to health social movement organizations? In fact, it would be unwise to use this framework uncritically to understand the environmental, antiwar, or globalization movements because the motivations underlying goals and strategies differ. Self-help organizations might engage in lobbying or use other overtly conventional political tactics, but they would not and could not launch a protest like that aimed at the G-8 summits. Still, both self-help and Greenpeace depend on legitimation and must manage their resources in an effective manner. This means that how and why members promote organizational legitimation, engage in political struggles and manage resources might differ in a fundamental way among movements, but *that* they do, does not.

While this line of argument suggests that the focus of the analyses discounts individuals, I have in fact included a discussion of a few key figures connected to several organizations in Chapter Four. In this chapter, group founders and leaders and movement entrepreneurs and activists, as well as their supporters and detractors emerged in a series of profiles that illustrate how health social movements like self-help engage in legitimation contests in order to thrive. A comprehensive analysis of individual leaders and their constituent groups would identify and follow their careers and influences and help us understand anomalies at the aggregate level such as that related to medical legitimation and self-help formation.

The next limitation is related to the first. It regards the conceptualization of self-help as a social movement generally and a health social movement in particular. What is problematic is that the social movement research framework itself is undergoing a series of transformations that raise the question of the definitional elements of the very subject of study (see Snow 2004). There is consequently no agreement on what is or is not a social movement, its elements, and actions. In addition, even self-help advocates, such as Alfred Katz (1993) are not sure whether self-help is a movement or not. Clearly, self-help organizations are unique kinds of collective actors. As suggested above, critics of self-help in particular and new social movements in general are quick to point out that joining a movement (such as the environmental or antiglobalization movement) with the goal of bringing about social justice, providing public services, challenging legal statutes and the like, is a fundamentally different activity than going to meetings of the National Alliance for the Mentally Ill or The Compassionate Friends. But movements tend to get defined based on a few characteristics, not the multiplicity of differences. For example, Wuthnow's (1994) study of the so-called small-group movement (SGM) consists of Christian and agnostic, self-help and neighborhood, couples' and literary types of organizations, among others. They are conceptually linked because they are small, community-based organizations. The question is: what does his analysis of SGM and my analysis of self-help gloss over by treating diverse types of social entities as a unified phenomenon? Certainly, individual variation tends to get slighted. Yet, the more important question is whether statements about groups and networks and organizations remain true when social entity A, such as self-help, is analyzed as if it were of a kind of social entity B. With regard to the present research question, how does self-help finesse legitimation and resources in route to becoming a way of life? Treating self-help, its constituents, leaders, bystander publics, and the rest like other health social movement organizations provides leverage that is missing from a focus on its unique characteristics. I argue that, given that self-help fits within some definitions of health social movements (even those that are overtly politically motivated), we can assume that it is, apply the appropriate framework, and empirically test the results. If analysis of self-help shows results similar to tests done on disparate organizations then there is evidence that our assumption is correct. If it does not show similar results, then the analyses may be incorrect, or the underlying assumptions may be incorrect. In my analysis, results indicate that like other health movements, self-help has access to and uses legitimating authority even as it opposes the grounds for that authority (Brown et al. 2004). Moreover, some forms of self-help resemble religious social movements and some resemble women's and gay rights movements. The open question is whether strategies for system change differ enough to characterize self-help and other social movement organizations along some dimension of "opposition-ness," especially in the latter two instances, where women's reproductive health and AIDS play a crucial role in larger movement strategies. That some self-help organizations may have more institutional access than Greenpeace, but less than, say the Sierra Club, suggests further lines of inquiry.

Assuming that self-help does resemble other kinds of health social movements and movements in general, its results are generalizable to them. Unfortunately, because the study of self-help as a movement is an emerging research project we have little to go on in the way of empirical comparison. So, conclusions based on any similarities or differences are provisional. In addition, the question remains whether health social movements are in turn similar to other kinds of social movements as such. That is, does the antismoking movement or the 1980s protests for AIDS funding parallel campaigns by other social movements for economic justice? Again, the health movement framework is still emerging. Consequently, the grounds for empirical comparison are preliminary. Using self-help as an example, while I am able to analyze which sociopolitical authorities are the most important for the survival and disbanding of self-help organizations, I do not explore the implications of these strategies for sociopolitical opportunities generally because how opportunities translate for an identity group as opposed to one oriented toward (political) legislative change remains unknown (see Snow 2004). For comparative purposes, future research can and should examine how sociopolitical opportunities and professional and political alliances among movement and institutional actors foster legitimation and promote the institutionalization of social movement practices regardless of strategic orientation.

Another limitation that needs to be recognized and one that is not unrelated to comparisons with other health movements concerns the use of national self-help organizations to investigate self-help. I have partially addressed the issue in Chapter Three. I examine national self-help/mutual-aid organizations because they were easier to identify, follow over time, and systematically analyze than local informal groups, since informal groups emerge and dissipate rapidly before they can be tracked. This suggests that my selection of analytic units is skewed in that it contains self-help organizations that are by definition more formalized, more legitimate, and possibly more dissimilar to grassroots social movement organizations. Combining these data with studies of local informal groups should generate a comprehensive picture of self-help at various stages, and I strongly encourage the project.

One last shortcoming concerns the implications of self-help's institutionalization for other social institutions. While the story I tell outlines the growth and institutionalization of self-help, it does not discuss its social, cultural, political, and economic effects. For example, Peele (1989) argues that the recovery movement has created a vast treatment industry, based on the erroneous premise that substance abuse is a disease and not a defect of personality. The point of his complaint though is not just the erroneous assumption of underlying addiction causation, but the puzzle of how a marginalized practice represented in some literatures as *retreatist*—the local twelve-step group—became a significant force within the billion-dollar treatment industry. To pursue this dilemma involves investigating how healthcare organizations and health social movements shape and are shaped by institutions beyond the healthcare sector.

Future Research

To imagine such a project, it is necessary to remember that I borrow descriptions from Scott et al. (2000) and Starr (1982) of the deinstitutionalization and fragmentation of mainstream healthcare in order to explain the conditions leading to the emergence and institutionalization of self-help. I do not examine the entire field of alternative healthcare nor analyze changes in mainstream healthcare itself, but look at the dynamics of one of the sector's most persistent organizational populations. It begins to answer the question of how marginal practices (self-help) became the basis for the practice of alternative services and begs the question why some of these practices have become integrated into formal organizational settings. For example, the recovery movement has brought about the widespread use of the twelve-step program of the anonymous groups in formal clinical settings. How does this happen and what are the institutional forces that influence this process?

Moreover, what social and cultural factors other that legitimation and resource use shape the development of alternative practices? A larger project should examine what other social movements and organizational sectors were involved in the deinstitutionalization and restructuring of mainstream healthcare. Examination of cross-movement relationships, along with a widening of the scope of outcomes to include processes of organizational diversification, as well as formation and failure, would provide much-needed insight into the social conditions shaping populations in multiple sectors. Since capturing the dynamics of institutionalization of collective phenomena remains a major goal in the social sciences (Friedland and Alford 1991), formulating and testing general theoretical propositions with different sectors is key to explaining institutional divergence (and congruence) of sectors.

Sociopolitical opportunities, cultural processes, and infrastructure are likely to have differential effects on health social movement formation and success in varying institutional contexts and through the course of the development of the population. For example, an explanatory scheme that would fit in with the previous discussion of national self-help organizations is Goldner's (2001) argument that changes in healthcare financing, consumer interest (i.e., demand), and government recognition (i.e., legitimacy) foster changing political opportunities that result in a bifurcation of complementary and alternative medicine (CAM) movement collective identity. On the one side are the alternative CAM proponents and on the other side are the integrationists. Increasingly, integrationists are gaining prominence. Political opportunities arise when elites, primarily physicians, make themselves available to the movement. How does it work? 1) Market mechanisms frustrate physicians deprived of authority, and consumers deprived of choice, and makes for potential collusion between them and 2) frustration increases demand for alternatives, but more importantly, consumers believe CAM is more effective for chronic conditions, which increases demand in its own right. To test this framework, we could imagine a selection of alternative healthcare providers with matching sociopolitical data. In short, an ecology of the field of alternative healthcare including other actors and populations could be used to test how political and market mechanisms influence the production space of complementary and alternative practices. Or, we could use this framework and analysis to examine the extent to which marginalized practices have become integrated into mainstream practices.

One question that remains open concerns the implications of the institutionalization of alternative practices. What does it mean when health movement organizations such as self-help become institutionalized? Since self-help itself is a formerly marginalized set of practices, how do other challengers deal with self-help once it becomes authoritative? For instance, formal organizations in the treatment industry have developed policy around innovations first used by self-help recovery organizations (White 1998), and act as recruitment mechanisms for these very same organizations, which in effect enhances their recognition, legitimacy, and power. Does this increase their capacity for effective performance? What are the institutional conditions that regulate industries that arose first as social movements, such as addiction recovery?

It has been important to analyze self-help organizations not only because they embody the preeminent social technology for resocialization and integration of select stigmatized populations but because health movements generate diversity, innovation, and social change. They contribute to pluralism by fostering sources of influence for disenfranchised groups that are not bound by state or market (DiMaggio and Anheier 1990). In contrast to these Tocquevillean sentiments, health movements may simply be sources of offloading for states' insoluble problems, which states support to avoid delegitimation (Offe 1985). Study of the rise of a population of organizations, such as self-help, particularly through analysis of institutional and organizational variation, provides insight into sociopolitical processes such as these. An organizations-social movement theoretical framework provides analysis of institutionalization of civil society organizational forms because of its ability to model socioeconomic and political processes as the intersection of interests originating in the domains of market, state, and culture at large. In an important sense, the study of diverse health movement populations provides a context for understanding how different organizational forms signal shifts in the composition of different versions of civil society, and the role organizational dynamics play in expansion of this sphere: an ongoing development for over the past hundred years in this country, and one just beginning in many others. The availability of self-help and its uses elsewhere (e.g., in the form of the worldwide spread of Alcoholics Anonymous models of temperance) underscores the possibilities for the direction of dramatic social change. The lessons learned here will therefore be all the more important for the future growth of societies that are now witnessing dramatic changes in their civil institutions.

Appendix A

Sources of Legitimation and Competition

Legitimation

Sources of Organizational Reputation (1955–2000)

Medical—National Library of Medicine, Index Medicus (4,300 periodicals e.g., New England Journal of Medicine, Journal of the American Medical Association, International Journal of Psychiatric Medicine, Journal of Consulting Clinical Psychology)

Academic—Sociological and Psychological Abstracts (2,500 and 1,300 periodicals, respectively e.g., American Sociological Review, American Journal of Sociology, Psychological Bulletin, Psychological Assessment, Journal of Community Psychology)

Political—Congressional Universe/ Congressional Information Services (CIS subject index of all regularly produced publications including hearings, testimony, reports e.g., House Interior and Insular Affairs Committee, Department of Labor, Department of Health and Human Services, Department of Education and Related Agencies for Appropriations)

Popular—New York Times Index (subject index)

Competition

Services (partial listing of over 300 services)

Children's services	Research Programs
Education network	Social Gatherings
Educational	Special Events/Social Events

Local and regional forums
Mother mentoring
Networking opportunities
Nutritional Programs
Referral services

Study groups
Supports research
Training Sessions
Training-employment skills
Transportation

Technologies

Advocacy

Charity fundraisers
Clearinghouse

Consultation

General outreach
General support networks
Information
Meetings, and discussion
  groups

Psychological, peer counseling,
  visitation programs
Public information
Seminars workshops
  conferences forums
Social recreational special
  events
Speaker bureau
Special programs
Statistics

Membership

Caretakers
Civic, religious, social

Clergy
Co-dependents
Concerned individuals
Counselors
Educators
Ex-spouses
Family members,
  relatives
Friends
Guidance workers

Hospitals
Human service

Law enforcement
Lay people
Legal professional
Libraries
Medical professionals
Other groups
Others

Parents
Partners

Personnel
Person w/ problem
  or stigma
Public
Researchers
Siblings
Social workers
Spouses
Staff
Students

Student unions
Survivor
Volunteer

Notes

I The Demography of Self-Help

1. Jane Mansbridge's 1980 study of the Help-Line Clinic in *Beyond Adversary Democracy* is an excellent ethnography of the day-to-day activities of one such organization.

2. Here and throughout the book I use institution to refer to rules, norms, and scripts for behavior, including conventions and practices and knowledge, which characterize a particular domain of activity such as the economy, politics, religion, science, medicine, and even popular culture (Scott 2001). Institutional authorities are those whose activities in a particular situation are consistent with maintaining practices of an institutional domain. In contrast, social movements seek institutional change.

3. In the following chapters I answer these and other questions. For instance, how many national self-help organizations are there? Almost six hundred over the course of 45 years, many with thousands of affiliated local chapters. What conditions do they treat? Everything from autism to Wegener's. How long do they last and who supports them? On average, they last about 15 years and they are supported not only popularly but also by medical professionals and academics. And, what kinds of resources do they use? They vie with one another for services in three hundred areas including transportation, study groups, nutritional programs, mother mentoring, special events/social events, educational training, employment skills, education network, networking, among others.

4. The exceptions include Davison, Pennebaker, and Dickerson (2000); Leventhal et al. (1988); Luke, Roberts, and Rappaport (1994); Maton (1993); Maton (1989); and Wituk et al. (2002), which I discuss throughout the book.

5. Unlike commercial populations, self-help differs, in one way, in that the main historical trend is away from increasing specialization of member interests, and generalist concentration, toward greater generalism (i.e., more inclusive, broader member interests) among organizations (see Chapter Three).

6. Examination of self-help organizational literature confirms that these organizations are purposive (goal-oriented) and sustained by a structure of roles (e.g., treasurers, committees, service board members, sponsors, secretaries, group chairpersons, and so on).

7. The National Alliance for the Mentally Ill is now known as the National Alliance on Mental Illness. I refer to it using its former title because of its familiarity.

8. For a social movement analogue see McAdam's (1999) notion of "cognitive liberation"—the ability to challenge what constitutes legitimate power in a *political* arena.

9. This definition of institution and institutionalization conflates the moral dimension of institutions with the taken-for-granted aspect of them (Suchman 1995). In this study, I follow the ecologists and focus on the processes of institutionalization as growing taken-for-grantedness, regardless of appropriateness, since social movement activity under some circumstances may be regarded as not appropriate but still taken-for-granted.

2 Defining Self-Help: How Does a Movement Become an Institution?

1. I discuss case selection criteria and the construction of the database in the following chapter.

2. Ruggie is referring to complementary and alternative medicine generally but these three ideas apply to the self-help movement. Self-help itself is an important actor in the promotion of complementary and alternative medicine.

3. Cf. Friedson (1970) on this point, who argues that in the context of how individuals legitimately enact the sick role. They may become ex-addicts or ex-cancer patients, but always remain "ex's." That self-help since the 1970s has managed to change how people think about addicts and cancer patients is testimony to its influence.

4. Although Abraham refers to EST as self-help, EST is not self-help in my definitional sense because it is organized by professionals rather than beneficiaries and members. However, its focus on face-to-face self-help and mutual-aid activities that take place in a therapeutic setting make it useful for understanding the ideological precursors of self-help.

5. See Wagner 1997 for a comparable argument.

3 From Small Beginnings: Growth and Diversification

This chapter has been adapted from an article published in *Nonprofit and Voluntary Sector Quarterly* and republished with kind permission of Sage Publications.

1. Tertiary movements are organizational populations within the self-help movement. They are called tertiary movements although some self-help research refers to them as separate movements.

2. Of the 589 national self-help organizations in this study, 28 cases were formed prior to the 1955 observation period. These include Alcoholics Anonymous

(1935), Al-Anon (1951), Associated Blind (1938), Mended Hearts Club (1951), and other founders. I discuss these in the section on diversification.

3. The issue of organizational control remains a sticky one even with the extensive criteria used to select the cases. As one critic points out, Reach for Recovery, for example, began as a member-controlled self-help organization but was later coopted by medical professionals. The cross-listing in Madara includes Reach for Recovery under breast cancer support with a note that individual groups (not the formal organization itself) are member-owned.

4. For example, organizations include: Acoustic Neuroma Association (acoustic neuroma), Adoptee Birthparent Support Network, Adoptees in Search (adoption), Adult Children Anonymous World Service Organization (family/ friends of alcoholics), Agoraphobics in Motion (agoraphobia), Aid to Incarcerated Mothers (incarceration), National Depressive and Manic Depressive Association (depression), National Graves Disease Foundation (Graves Disease), Sjogren's Syndrome Foundation (Sjogren's Syndrome), Voices in Action (incest), We Can Do! (cancer), Wegener's Granulomatosis Support Group (genetic), Women for Sobriety (alcoholism), and Women Helping Women (divorce).

5. Please note, membership figures for voluntary associations are intractable. Trying to capture annual changes is challenging at best. Unfortunately, these are the only data currently available for self-help. I therefore omit cases with questionable and missing data from analyses of market share.

6. I also created a measure that examined *service-use* across membership levels. The idea was to test whether a limited constituency and few service offerings could be used to define specialist self-help while a broad-based constituency with many types of members and many services defined generalist self-help. This measure simply confirmed trends shown with the simpler tool, using membership only, so I retained the simple measure.

7. This may represent consolidation of a few powerful organizations such as Alcoholics Anonymous and Narcotics Anonymous.

8. These are the largest organizations because they have the most members.

9. Note that in 1955 Alcoholics Anonymous and Taking Off Pounds Sensibly had the largest share with about 730,000 members, compared to Narcotics Anonymous and National Amputee Foundation, with approximately 5,000 members each. In contrast, Al-Anon had 50,000, Mended Hearts 24,000, International Association of Larynectomees 24,000, and Spinal Cord Foundation 5,000.

4 Legitimation: The Paradox of Public Recognition of Self-Help

Portions of this chapter have been adapted from an article published in *The International Journal of Sociology and Social Policy* and republished with kind permission of Emerald Publications Inc.

1. The fittest organizations are those whose structures, practices, and sociopolitical connections assure their survival. In this case, these consist in legitimation and control of resources.

2. Parents Anonymous 2005. www.parentsanonymous.org/pahtml/paMHabout. html. Accessed on June 30, 2005.
3. Medline www.ncbi.nlm.nih.gov/entrez. Accessed on June 14, 2005.
4. Later in this chapter, we will see the same pattern repeated in Depression after Delivery, where postpartum depression is linked to infanticide.
5. Today it is known as First Candle/National SIDS Alliance.
6. Http://www.nami org/ Template.cfm?section=your_local_NAMI. Accessed on October 14, 2005.

5   The Evolution of Public Recognition and Its Consequences

1. In some sense, measures of congressional appearances, lobby efforts, and interactions with elites represent alliances between self-help and political authorities (see Bergman's 1986 discussion for example). Since these alliances produce legitimacy, I use them in these analyses as indicators of legitimation. Elsewhere, I have used them as measures of self-help—political affiliation.
2. One of the limitations of this study is that at the time of data gathering (1997–2000), it was impossible to obtain and code the hundreds and hundreds of articles for strength of support or hostility toward self-help. A sample of articles, however, revealed that very few were critical of self-help and even the critical ones tended to maintain a stance of scientific neutrality. Books about self-help, not included in these counts, are a different matter. See below.
3. Self-help has generated its share of ideological hostility, for example, Greenberg 1994; Kaminer 1992; Peele 1989; Rapping 1996; Rieff 1991; and Wagner 1997 have all taken a critical position. Interestingly, while these critiques have questioned the appropriateness and effectiveness of self-help for treating certain conditions, their overall impact on the acceptance of self-help has been limited.
4. In fig. 5.1, I have used adjusted indicators for trends in public recognition. These are constructed by dividing the number of articles by the size of the organizational population in each period. In fig. 5.2, I use unadjusted, raw numbers to show the real amount of recognition. There are trade-offs between using the two. The unadjusted figures yield the actual number of public references to self-help. The adjusted rates yield an average amount. I include the adjusted rates because of the confounding influence of population size. That is, there will be an increase in the amount of recognition self-help achieves simply because of increases in the sheer volume of organizations. Adjusted rates depict trends in the "average" legitimation rate over time, which would guarantee that it is not dependent on growth in the size of the population.
5. I use the raw unadjusted rates here to show the actual numbers of articles, stories, and congressional appearances that indicate public recognition, since looking at each specialty area controls for population-size differences.
6. Note however, that this relationship may be due to other unmeasured factors.

6   Resources: How Competition Selects Only the Fittest Organizations

1. The difference "d" is just a heuristic for calculating the ratio of niche overlap to non-overlap:

$$d(i,j) = \frac{a_{i,j}}{a_{i,j} + b_{i,j} + c_{i,j}} / N_j \tag{1}$$

where the proportionate difference (d) between a focal organization (i) and the other organizations sharing its particular niche (j) (e.g., marriage and family, infant mortality), is a function of the overlap $(a_{i,j})$ of services, social technologies and membership, relative to $a_{i,j}$ plus $b_{i,j}$ plus $c_{i,j}$; where "b" represents services, social technologies and membership of the focal organization (i), relative to another organization; and "c" represents the services, social technologies, and membership of another organization relative to the focal organization (i). The calculation for the quantities $a_{i,j}$ or $b_{i,j}$ or $c_{i,j}$ is the same. For instance: $a_{i,j} = \sum a_{i+1,j}, a_{i+2,j}, a_{i+3,j} \ldots a_{+ki,j}$. The algorithm then averages over all the organizations in the niche (N_j) and calculates the median level of resource overlap in the population at time t.
2. In actuality, all groups held meetings, so overlap is between remaining types of social technologies.
3. It is a rate insofar as it is the number of failed organizations *per year*.

7   Conclusion and Future Directions

1. See Armstrong 2002, for a discussion of this same process in the gay rights movement.

Book References

Abraham, Gary. 1988. The protestant ethic and the spirit of utilitarianism: the case of EST. *Theory and Society* 12:739–774.

Alcoholics Anonymous. 2005. New York: AA World Services.

Aldrich, Howard E. 1999. *Organizations Evolving*. Thousand Oaks, CA: Sage Publications.

Allsop, Judith, Kathryn Jones, and Rob Baggott. 2004. Health consumer groups in the UK: a new social movement? *Sociology of Health and Illness* 26 (6):737–756.

Archibald, Matthew E. 2004. Between isomorphism and market partitioning: how organizational competencies and resources foster cultural and sociopolitical legitimacy, and promote organizational survival in *Research in the Sociology of Organizations* edited by Cathryn Johnson, 22:171–211. Oxford, UK: JAI Press.

———. Forthcoming 2007. Growth, diversification and resource partitioning in alternative health and human services: an organizational ecology of self-help/mutual-aid in *Nonprofit and Voluntary Sector Quarterly*. Thousand Oaks, CA: Sage Publications.

———. Forthcoming 2007. The dilemma of legitimation in challenger organizations: public recognition of self-help/mutual-aid in *International Journal of Sociology and Social Policy* edited by Timothy J. Dowd. London: Emerald Publications Inc.

Armstrong, Elizabeth A. 2002. *Forging gay identities : organizing sexuality in San Francisco, 1950–1994*. Chicago: University of Chicago Press.

Barron, David N. 1999. The structuring of organizational populations. *American Sociological Review* 64:421–446.

Bartalos, Michael K. 1992. Illness, professional caregivers and self-helpers in *Self-Help: Concepts and Applications* edited by Alfred H. Katz, Hannah L. Hedrick, Daryl Holtz Isenberg, Leslie M. Thompson, Therese Goodrich, and Austin H. Kutscher, 68–75. Philadelphia, PA: Charles Press.

Baum, Joel A.C. 1996. Organizational ecology in *Handbook of Organizations Studies* edited by Stewart R. Clegg, Cynthia Hardy, and Walter R. Nord, 77–114. Thousand Oaks, CA: Sage Publications.

Baum, Joel A.C. and Christine Oliver. 1996. Toward an institutional ecology of organizational founding. *Academy of Management Journal* 39:1378–1427.

Beattie, Melodie. 1987. *Co-Dependent No More: How to Stop Controlling Others and Care for Yourself*. New York: Harper-Hazelden.

Bergman, Abraham. 1986. *The Discovery of Sudden Infant Death Syndrome: Lessons in the Practice of Political Medicine*. New York: Praeger.

Boli, John, and George Thomas. 1999. INGOs and the organization of world culture in *Constructing World Culture* edited by John Boli and George M. Thomas, 13–49. Stanford, CA: Stanford University Press.

Boone, Christophe, Glenn R. Carroll, and Arjen van Witteloostuijn. 2002. Resource distributions and market partitioning: Dutch daily newspapers, 1968 to 1994. *American Sociological Review* 67:408–431.

Borkman, Thomasina. 1991. Introduction. *American Journal of Community Psychology* 19(5):643–650.

———. 1999. *Understanding Self-Help/Mutual-Aid : Experiential Learning in the Commons*. New Brunswick, NJ: Rutgers University Press.

Borman, Leonard. 1992. Introduction: self-help/mutual-aid groups in strategies for health in *Self-Help: Concepts and Applications* edited by Alfred H. Katz, Hannah L. Hedrick, Daryl Holtz Isenberg, Leslie M. Thompson, Therese Goodrich, and Austin H. Kutscher, xix–xxvii. Philadelphia, PA: Charles Press.

Bradshaw, John. 1988. *Bradshaw on the Family*. Deerfield Beach, FL.: Health Communications.

Brown, Phil and Stephen Zavestoski. 2004. Social movements in health: an introduction. *Sociology of Health and Illness* (6):679–694.

Brown, Phil, Stephen Zavestoski, Sabrina McCormick, Brian Mayer, Rachel Morello-Frosch, and Rebecca Gasior Altman. 2004. Embodied health movements: new approaches to social movements in health. *Sociology of Health and Illness* 26:1–31.

Campbell, John L. 2005. Where do we stand? Common mechanisms in organizations and social movements research in *Social Movements and Organization Theory* edited by Gerald F. Davis, Doug McAdam, W. Richard Scott, and Mayer N. Zald, 41–68. New York: Cambridge University Press.

Carroll, Glenn R. 1985. Concentration and specialization: dynamics of niche width in populations of organizations. *American Sociological Review* 100:720–749.

Carroll, Glenn R. and Ananda Swaminathan. 2000. Why the microbrewery movement? Organizational dynamics of resource partitioning in the American brewing industry after probation. *American Journal of Sociology* 106:715–762.

Carroll, Glenn R. and Michael T. Hannan. 2000. *The Demography of Corporations and Industries*. Princeton, NJ: Princeton University Press.

Carroll, Glenn R., Stanislav D. Dobrev, and Anand Swaminathan. 2003. Organizational processes of resource partitioning in *Research in Organizational Behavior* edited by Barry M. Staw and R.M. Kramer, 24:1–40. New York: JAI/Elsevier.

Charmaz, Kathy. 2000. Experiencing chronic illness in *The Handbook of Social Studies in Health and Medicine* edited by Gary Albrecht, Ray Fitzpatrick, and Susan Scrimshaw, 277–292. London: Sage Publications.

Clemens, Elizabeth. 1996. Organizational form as frame: collective identity and political strategy in the American labor movement, 1880–1920 in *Comparative*

Perspectives on Social Movements edited by Doug McAdam, John D. McCarthy, and Mayer N. Zald, 205–226. New York: Cambridge University Press.

Cohen, Jean and Andrew Arato. 1992. *Civil Society and Political Theory.* Cambridge, MA: MIT Press.

Congressional Universe/Congressional Information Services, 1955–2000 (CIS subject index).

Conrad, Peter. 1992. Medicalization and social control. *Annual Review of Sociology* 18:209–232.

Cress, Daniel M. and Daniel J. Myers. 2004. Introdution: Authority in contention in *Authority in Contention Vol 25 Research in Social Movements, Conflict and Change* edited by Daniel J. Myers and Daniel M. Cress, xi–xxiii. Oxford: JAI Press.

Davison, Kathryn P., James W. Pennebaker, and Sally S. Dickerson. 2000. Who talks? The social psychology of illness support groups. *American Psychologist* 55:205–217.

Denzin, Norman K. 1987. *The Recovering Alcoholic.* Newbury Park, CA: Sage Publications.

DiMaggio, Paul J., and Helmut K. Anheier. 1990. The sociology of nonprofit organizations and sectors. *Annual Review of Sociology* 16:137–159.

DiMaggio, Paul J. and Walter W. Powell. 1983. The iron cage revisited: Institutional isomorphism and collective rationality. *American Sociological Review* 48:147–160.

Donaldson, Lex. 1996. The normal science of structural contingency theory in *Handbook of Organization Studies* edited by Stewart R. Clegg, Cynthia. Hardy, and Walter. R. Nord, 57–77. London: Sage Publications.

Dowd, Timothy J. 2004. Concentration and diversity revisited: production logics and the U.S. mainstream recording market, 1940–1990. *Social Forces* 82:1411–1457.

Duggan, Lisa and Nan D. Hunter. 1995. *Sex Wars: Sexual Dissent and Political Culture.* New York: Routledge.

Fligstein, Neil N. 1998. Fields, power, and social skill: a critical analysis of the new institutionalisms. Paper presented at Hamburg University October 9–11, 1997.

Fombrun, Charles. J. 1996. *Reputation: Realizing Value from the Corporate Image.* Boston: Harvard Business School Press.

Freidson, Eliot. 1970. *Profession of Medicine: A Study of the Sociology of Applied Knowledge.* Chicago: University of Chicago Press.

Friedland, Roger, and Robert R. Alford. 1991. Bringing society back in: symbols, practices, and institutional contradictions in *The New Institutionalism in Organizational Analysis* edited by Walter W. Powell and Paul J. DiMaggio, 232–267. Chicago, IL: University of Chicago Press.

Gale Research Company. 1955–2000. *Encyclopedia of Associations, Vol. 1–36, National Organizations.* Detroit, MI: Gale Research.

Gamson, William A. 1975. *The Strategy of Social Protest.* Belmont CA: Wadsworth.

Gamson, William A. and David S. Meyer. 1996. Framing political opportunity in *Comparative Perspectives on Social Movements: Political Opportunities, Mobilizing Structures, and Cultural Framings* edited by Doug McAdam, John

D. McCarthy, and Mayer N. Zald, 275–290. New York: Cambridge University Press.

Goffman, Ernest. 1963. *Stigma*. Englewood Cliffs, NJ: Prentice Hall.

Goldner, Melinda. 2001. Expanding political opportunities and changing collective identities in the complementary and alternative medicine movement in *Research in Social Movements, Conflicts and Change* edited by Patrick G. Coy, 69–102. Oxford, UK: Elsevier Science.

Goldstein, Michael S. 1992. *The Health Movement: Promoting Fitness in America*. New York: Twayne Publishers.

Greenberg, Gary. 1994. *The Self on the Shelf: Recovery Books and the Good Life*. New York: State University of New York Press.

Greenleaf, Jael. 1987. *Co-Alcoholic, Para-Alcoholic: Who's Who and What's the Difference?* New Orleans: Mac Publications.

Haider-Markel, Donald P. 1997. Interest group survival: shared interests versus competition for resources. *The Journal of Politics* 59:903–912.

Hall, Peter Dobkin. 1992. *Inventing the Non-Profit Sector and Other Essays on Philanthropy, Voluntarism, and Nonprofit Organizations*. Baltimore, Maryland: Johns Hopkins University Press.

Hannan, Michael T. 1998. Rethinking age dependence in organizational mortality: logical formalizations. *American Journal of Sociology* 104:85–123.

Hannan, Michael T. and John H. Freeman. 1977. The population ecology of organizations. *American Journal of Sociology* 82:929–964.

———. 1989. *Organizational Ecology*. Cambridge: Harvard University Press.

Hedrick, Hannah L., Daryl Holtz Isenberg, and Martini. 1992. Self-help groups: empowerment through policy and partnerships in *Self-Help: Concepts and Applications* edited by Alfred H. Katz, Hannah L. Hedrick, Daryl Holtz Isenberg, Leslie M. Thompson, Therese Goodrich, and Austin H. Kutscher, 1–25. Philadelphia, PA: Charles Press.

Humphreys, Keith and Julian Rappaport. 1993. Researching self-help/mutual-aid groups and organizations: many roads, one journey. *Applied and Preventive Psychology* 3:217–231.

Humphreys, Keith and Lee Ann Kaskutas. 1995. World views of alcoholics anonymous, women for sobriety and adult children of alcoholics/al-anon mutual help groups. *Addiction Research* 3:231–243.

Hurvitz, Nathan. 1976. The origins of peer self-help psychotherapy group movement. *The Journal of Applied Behavioral Science* 12:283–294.

Illinois Self-Help Coalition.1997. www.selfhelp-illinois.org. Accessed August 1, 2000.

Index Medicus, National Library of Medicine, 1955–2000.

Jepperson, Ronald L. 1991. Institutions, institutional effects, and institutionalism in *The New Institutionalism in Organizational Analysis* edited by Walter W. Powell and Paul J. DiMaggio, 143–164. Chicago, IL: University of Chicago Press.

———. 2002. The development and application of sociological neoinstitutionalism in *New Directions in Contemporary Sociological Theory* edited by Joseph Berger and Morris Zelditch Jr. Lanham, 229–267. Maryland: Rowman and Littlefield Publishers, Inc.

Joffe, Carole E., Tracy A. Weitz, and Claire L. Stacey. 2004. Uneasy allies: pro-choice physicians, feminist health activists and the struggle for abortion rights. *Sociology of Health and Illness* 26 (6):775–796.

Johnson, Michael P. and Karl Hufbauer. 2003. Sudden infant death syndrome and a medical research problem since 1945 in *Health and Health Care as Social Problems* edited by Peter Conrad and Valerie Leiter, 87–106. Lanham, Maryland: Rowman and Littlefield.

Kaminer, Wendy. 1992. *I'm Dysfunctional, You're Dysfunctional: The Recovery Movement and Other Self-Help Fashions*. Reading, MA: Addison-Wesley.

Katz, Alfred H. 1993. *Self-Help in America: A Social Movement Perspective*. New York: Twayne.

——. 1992a. Professional/self-help group relationships: general issues in *Self-Help Concepts and Applications* edited by Alfred H. Katz, Hannah L. Hedrick, Daryl Holtz Isenberg, Leslie M. Thompson, Therese Goodrich, and Austin H. Kutscher, 56–61. Philadelphia, PA: Charles Press.

——. 1992b. Introduction in *Self-Help Concepts and Applications* edited by Alfred H. Katz, Hannah L. Hedrick, Daryl Holtz Isenberg, Leslie M. Thompson, Therese Goodrich, and Austin H. Kutscher, 1–25. Philadelphia, PA: Charles Press.

Katz, Alfred H. and Eugene I. Bender. 1976. Self-help groups in western society: history and prospects. *The Journal of Applied Behavioral Science* 12:265–282.

Kauffman, L.A. 1995. Small change: radical politics since the 1960s in *Cultural Politics and Social Movements* edited by Marcy Darnovsky, Barbara Epstein, and Richard Flacks, 1–25. Philadelphia: Temple University Press.

Klawiter, Maren. 2004. Breast cancer in two regimes: the impact of social movements on illness experience. *Sociology of Health and Illness* 26(6):845–874.

Knoke, David. 1986. Associations and interest groups. *Annual Review of Sociology* 12:1–21.

——. 1989. Resource acquisition and allocation in U.S. national associations in *International Social Movement Research* edited by Bert Klandermans, 129–154. Oxford, UK: JAI Press Inc.

Kriesi, Hans Peter. 1996. The organizational structure of new social movements in a political context in *Comparative Perspectives on Social Movements: Political Opportunities, Mobilizing Structures, and Cultural Framings* edited by Doug McAdam, John D. McCarthy, and Mayer N. Zald, 152–184. New York: Cambridge University Press.

Kurtz, Ernest. 1979. *Not-God: A History of Alcoholics Anonymous*. Hazelden, MN: Educational Services.

Kurtz, Linda Farris. 1997. *Self-Help and Support Groups: A Handbook for Practitioners*. Thousand Oaks, CA: Sage Publications.

Ladd, Everett C. 1998. Bowling with Tocqueville: Civic Engagement and Social Capital. American Enterprise Institute for Public Policy and Research Bradley Lecture, September 15, available at http://www.aei.org/bradley/b1091598.html. Accessed September 7, 2001.

Lasch, Christopher. 1984. *The Minimal Self: Psychic Survival in Troubled Times*. New York: W.W. Norton and Company.

Lee, Judith A.B. and Carol R. Swenson. 1994. The concept of mutual aid in *Mutual Aid Groups, Vulnerable Populations, and the Life Cycle*, 2nd edition edited by Alexa Gitterman and Lawrence Shulman, 413–431. New York: Columbia University Press.

Leventhal, Gerald S., Kenneth I. Maton, and Edward J. Madara. 1988. Systematic organizational support for self-help groups. *American Journal of Orthopsychiatry* 58:592–603.

Lieberman, Morton A. and Lonnie R. Snowden. 1994. Problems in assessing prevalence and membership characteristics of self-help group participants in *Understanding the Self-Help Organization: Frameworks and Findings* edited by Thomas J. Powell, 32–49. Thousand Oaks, CA: Sage Publications.

Luke, Douglas A., Linda Roberts, and Julian Rappaport. 1994. Individual, group context and individual-group fit predictors of self-help group attendance in *Understanding the Self-Help Organization: Frameworks and Findings* edited by Thomas J. Powell, 88–115. Thousand Oaks, CA: Sage Publications.

Makela, Klaus, Ilkka Arminen, Kim Bloomfield, Irmgard Eisenbach-Stangl, Karin Helmersson Bergmark, Noriko Kurube, et al. 1996. *Alcoholics Anonymous as a Mutual-Help Movement:A Study in Eight Societies*. Wisconsin: University of Wisconsin Press.

Maino D.M., J. Kofman, M.F. Flynn, and L. Lai. 1994. Ocular manifestations of sotos syndrome. *Journal of the American Optometric Association* 65(5):339–346.

Mansbridge, Jane J. 1980. *Beyond Adversary Democracy*. Chicago: University of Chicago Press.

Margrab, Phyllis R. and Hillary E.C. Millar. 1989. Proceedings of the surgeon general's conference March 13–15, 1989, available at http://hctransitions.ichp.edu/1989conf/conf89.pdf. Accessed May 12, 2000.

Martin, Andrew W., Frank Baumgartner, and John D. McCarthy. 2005. Measuring association populations using the encyclopedia of associations: evidence from the field of labor unions. *Social Science Research* 35: 771–778.

Marx, Gary T. and Douglas McAdam. 1994. *Collective Behavior and Social Movements:Process and Structure*. New Jersey: Prentice Hall, Inc.

Maton, Kenneth I. 1993. Moving beyond the individual level of analysis in mutual help group research: an ecological paradigm. *Journal of Applied Behavioral Science* 29:272–286.

———. 1989. Towards an ecological understanding of mutual-help groups: the social ecology of "fit." *American Journal of Community Psychology* 17:729–753.

McAdam, Doug. 1999. *Political Process and the Development of Black Insurgency, 1930–1970*. 2nd edition. Chicago, IL.: The University of Chicago Press.

McAdam, Doug, John D. McCarthy, and Mayer N. Zald. 1988. Social movements in *Handbook of Sociology* edited by Neil J. Smelser, 695–737. Newbury Park, CA: Sage Publications.

———.1996. Introduction: opportunities, mobilizing structures, and framing processes in *Comparative Perspectives on Social Movements: Political Opportunities, Mobilizing Structures, and Cultural Framings* edited by Doug McAdam, John McCarthy, and Mayer Zald, 1–22. Cambridge: Cambridge University Press.

McCarthy, John D. and Mayer N. Zald. 1994 [1977]. Resource mobilization and social movements: a partial theory in *Social Movements in an Organizational Society* edited by Mayer N. Zald and John D. McCarthy, 15–42. New Brunswick: Transaction.

McAdam, Doug, Sidney Tarrow, and Charles Tilly. 2001. *Dynamics of Contention.* Cambridge: Cambridge University Press.

McGee, Micki. 2005. *Self-Help, Inc.: Makeover Culture in American Life.* New York: Oxford University Press.

McPherson, Miller. 1983. An ecology of affiliation. *American Sociological Review* 48:519–532.

Meyer, David S. 2004. Protest and political opportunities. *Annual Review of Sociology* 30:125–145.

Meyer, David S. and Debra C. Minkoff. 2004. Conceptualizing political opportunity. *Social Forces* 82:1457–1492.

Meyer, David S. and Nancy Whittier. 1994. Social movement spillover. *Social Problems* 41:277–298.

Meyer, John W. 1977. The effects of education as an institution. *American Journal of Sociology* 83:53–77.

Meyer, John W. and Brian Rowan. 1977. Institutional organizations: formal structure as myth and ceremony. *American Journal of Sociology* 83(2):340–363.

Mezias, J. and S.J. Mezias. 2000. Resource partitioning, the founding of specialist firms, and innovation: the American feature film industry, 1912–1929. *Organization Science* 11:306–322.

Minkoff, Debra C. 1995. *Organizing for Equality: The Evolution of Women's and Racial-Ethnic Organizations in America, 1955–1985.* New Brunswick, NJ: Rutgers University Press.

———. 1994. From service provision to institutional advocacy: the shifting legitimacy of organizational forms. *Social Forces* 72:943–969.

Mullen, Fitzhugh. 1992. Rewriting the social contract in health in *Self-Help: Concepts and Applications* edited by Alfred H. Kat, Hannah L. Hedrick, Daryl Holtz Isenberg, Leslie M. Thompson, Therese Goodrich, and Austin H. Kutscher, 61–68. Philadelphia, PA: Charles Press.

Nash, Kermit B. and Kathryn D. Kramer. 1994. Self-help for sickle cell disease in African American communities in *Understanding the Self-Help Organization* edited by Thomas J. Powell, 212–227. Thousand Oaks, CA: Sage Publications.

New York Times Subject Index 1955–2000 .

North, Douglass. 1990. *Institutions, Institutional Change and Economic Performance.* Cambridge: Cambridge University Press.

Offe, Claus. 1985. New social movements: challenging the boundaries of institutional politics. *Social Research* 52:817–880.

Parents Anonymous Research Profile. 2000. Http://www.parentsanonymous.org/pahtml/pubPubs.html. Accessed January 20, 2007.

Parsons, Talcott. 1956. Suggestions for a sociological approach to the theory of organizations, Parts I and II. *Administrative Science Quarterly* 1:63–85.

Peele, Stanton M. 1989. *The Diseasing of America: Addiction Treatment Out of Control.* Lexington, MA: D.C. Heath.

Peindl K.S., K.L. Wisner, K.L.E.J. Zolnik, and B.H. Hanusa. 1995. Effects of post-partum depression on family planning international. *Journal of Psychiatry Medicine* 25(3):291–300.

Pfeffer, Jeffrey. 1997. *New Directions for Organization Theory*. New York: Oxford University Press.

Pfohl, Stephen J. 2003. The "discovery" of child abuse in *Health and Health Care as Social Problems* edited by Peter Conrad and Valerie Leiter, 69–86. Lanham, Maryland: Rowman and Littlefield.

Polletta, Francesca. 2004. Culture in and outside institutions in *Research in Social Movements, Conflicts, and Change. Special Issue, Authority in Contention* edited by Daniel J. Myers and Daniel M. Cress, 161–183. New York: Elsevier.

Popielarz, Pamela A. and Miller McPherson. 1995. On the edge or in between: niche position, niche overlap, and the duration of voluntary memberships. *American Journal of Sociology* 101:3, 696–720.

Powell, Thomas J. 1987. *Self-Help Organizations and Professional Practice*. Silver Spring, MD: National Association of Social Workers.

———. 1990. *Working with Self-Help*. Silver Spring, MD: NASW.

———. 1994. Introduction in *Understanding the Self-Help Organization* edited by Thomas J. Powell, 1–20. Thousand Oaks, CA: Sage Publications.

Putnam, Robert D. 2000. *The Collapse and Revival of American Community*. New York: Simon and Schuster.

Rao, Hayagreeva, Calvin Morrill, and Mayer Zald. 2000. Power plays: how social movements and collective action create new organizational forms in *Research in Organizational Behavior* edited by Barry Staw and Robert Sutton, 239–282. New York: Elsevier.

Rappaport, Julian. 1993. Narrative studies, personal stories and identity transformation in the context of mutual help. *Journal of Applied Behavioral Science* 29:237–254.

Rapping, Elayne. 1996. *The Culture of Recovery: Making Sense of the Self-Help Movement in Women's Lives*. Boston, MA: Beacon Press.

Rice, John Steadman. 1996. *A Disease of One's Own: Psychotherapy, Addiction, and the Emergence of Co-Dependency*. New Brunswick: Transaction Publishers.

Rieff, David. 1991. Victims all? Recovery, co-dependency and the art of blaming somebody else. *Harper's* Magazine October:49–56.

Rienarman, M. 1995. The twelve-step movement and advanced capitalist culture: the politics of self control in postmodernity in *Cultural Politics and Social Movements* edited by Marcy Darnovsky, Barbara Epstein, and Richard Flacks, 90–110. Philadelphia: Temple University Press.

Riessman, Frank. 1985. New dimensions in self-help. *Social Policy* 15:2–4.

Riessman, Frank and David Carroll. 1995. *Redefining Self-Help: Policy and Practice*. San Francisco, CA: Jossey-Bass.

Riessman, Frank and T. Bay. 1992. The politics of self-help. *Social Policy* 23(2):28–38.

Rudy, David R. and Arthur L. Greil. 1988. Is alcoholics anonymous a religious organization?: Meditations on marginality. *Sociological Analysis* 50:41–51.

Ruef, Martin, Peter Mendel, and W. Richard Scott. 1998. An organizational field approach to resource environments in healthcare: comparing hospitals and home health agencies in the San Francisco bay region. *Health Services Research* 32:775–803.

Ruggie, Mary. 2004. *Marginal to Mainstream: Alternative Medicine in America.* New York: Cambridge University Press.

Sandell, Rickard. 2001. Organizational growth and ecological constraints: the growth of social movements in Sweden, 1881 to 1940. *American Sociological Review* 66:672–693.

Schaeff, Ann Wilson. 1986. *Co-Dependence—Misunderstood-Mistreated.* New York: Harper and Row.

———. 1987. *When Society Becomes an Addict.* New York: Harper and Row.

Scheidlinger, Steven. 2000. The group psychotherapy movement at the millennium: Some historical perspectives. *International Journal of Group Psychotherapy* 50:315–339.

Schneiberg, Marc. 2002. Organizational heterogeneity and the production of new forms: politics, social movements and mutual companies in American fire insurance in *Research in the Sociology of Organizations* edited by Michael. Lounsbury and Marc Ventresca, 39–91. Oxford: JAI Press.

Schneiberg, Marc, and Sarah Soule. 2005. Institutionalization as a contested multilevel process: the case of rate regulation in American fire insurance in *Social Movements and Organization Theory* edited by Gerald F. Davis, Doug McAdam, W. Richard Scott, and Mayer N. Zald, 122–161. New York: Cambridge University Press.

Schubert, Marsha A. and Thomasina J. Borkman. 1991. An organizational typology for self-help. *American Journal of Community Psychology* 19:769–787.

Scott, W. Richard. 2003. *Organizations: Rational, Natural, and Open Systems.* 5th edition Thousand Oaks, CA: Sage Publications.

———. 2001. *Institutions and Organizations.* Thousand Oaks, CA: Sage Publications.

Scott, W. Richard, Martin Ruef, Peter J. Mendel, and Carol A. Caronna. 2000. *Institutional Change and Healthcare Organizations: From Professional Dominance to Managed Care.* Chicago: University of Chicago Press.

Self-Help Network http://www.selfhelpnetwork.wichita.edu. Accessed on November 20, 2000.

Shepherd, Matthew D. Mike Schoenberg, Susan Slavich, Scott Wituk, Mary Warren, and Greg Meissen. 1999. Continuum of professional involvement in self-help groups. *Journal of Community Psychology* 27:39–53.

Simonds, Wendy. 1992. *Women and Self-Help Culture: Reading between the Lines.* New Brunswick: Rutgers University Press.

Singh, Jitendra V., David J. Tucker, and Agnes G. Meinhard. 1991. Institutional change and ecological dynamics in *The New Institutionalism in Organizational Analysis* edited by Walter W. Powell and Paul J. DiMaggio, 361–390. Chicago, IL: University of Chicago Press.

Skocpol, Theda. 1996. Unraveling from above. *The American Prospect* 25:20–25.

Smith, David Horton and Karl Pillemer. 1983. Self-help groups as social movement organizations: social structure and social change in *Research in Social*

Movements, Conflicts and Change edited by Louis Kriesberg, 6:203–233. Greenwich, CT: JAI Press.

Smith, Steven Rathgeb and Michael Lipsky. 1993. *Nonprofits for Hire: The Welfare State in the Age of Contracting*. Cambridge, MA: Harvard University Press.

Snow, David A. 2004. Social movements as challenges to authority: resistance to an emerging conceptual hegemony in *Research in Social Movements, Conflicts, and Change. Special Issue, Authority in Contention*, edited by Daniel J. Myers and Daniel M. Cress, 3–25. New York: Elsevier.

Sociological and Psychological Abstracts 1955–2000.

Starr, Paul. 1982. *The Social Transformation of American Medicine: The Rise of a Sovereign Profession and the Making of a Vast Industry*. New York: Basic Books.

Stryker, Robin. 2000. Legitimacy process as institutional politics: implications for theory and research in the sociology of organizations in *Research in the Sociology of Organizations* Vol. 17 edited by Samuel Bacharach and Edward J. Lawler, 179–223. Greenwich, CT: JAI Press

Suchman, Mark C. 1995. Managing legitimacy: strategic and institutional approaches. *Academy of Management Review* 20:571–610.

Taylor, Verta A. 1996. *Rock-a-by Baby : Feminism, Self Help, and Postpartum Depression*. New York: Routledge.

Tilly, Charles. 2002. Comment on young buried gold. *American Sociological Review* 67:689–692.

Tocqueville, Alexis de. 1951. *De la democratie en amerique, tome second*. Paris: Editions M.-Th. Genin, Libraire de Medicis.

Tucker, David J., Jitendra V. Singh, Agnes G. Meinhard, and Robert J. House.1988. Ecological and institutional sources of change in organizational populations in *Ecological Models of Organizations* edited by Glenn Carroll, 127–152. Cambridge, MA: Ballinger.

Twombly, Eric C. 2003. What factors affect the entry and exit of nonprofit human service organizations in metropolitan areas? *Nonprofit and Voluntary Sector Quarterly* 32(2): 211–235.

U.S. Bureau of the Census. 2001. *Statistical Abstract of the United States*. Washington, DC: U.S. Government Printing Office.

U.S. Department of Health and Human Services. 1987. *Surgeon General's Workshop on Self-Help and Public Health*. Washington DC: U.S. Government Printing Office.

U.S. Department of Labor. 1999. *Social Security Bulletin*. Washington DC: U.S. Government Printing Office.

U.S. Department of Labor-Office of Education, National Center for Education Statistics. 1999. *HEGIS and IPEDS Surveys*. Washington DC: U.S. Government Printing Office.

Wagner, David. 1997. *The New Temperance: The American Obsession with Sin And Vice*. Boulder, CO: Westview Press.

Wegschieder-Cruse, Sharon.1984. *Co-Dependency: An Emerging Issue*. Deerfield Beach, Fla.: Health Communications.

Weitz, Rose. 2001. *The Sociology of Health, Illness, and Health Care*. Belmont, CA.: Wadsworth.

Wituk, Scott, Matthew Shepherd, Mary Warren, and Greg Meissen. 2002. "Factors contributing to the survival of self-help groups." *American Journal of Community Psychology* 30:349–366.

White, Barbara J. and Edward J. Madara. 2002. 7th edition. *The Self-Help Sourcebook: Finding and Forming Mutual Aid Self-Help Groups*. Denville, NJ: New Jersey Self-Help Clearinghouse.

White, William L. 1998. *Slaying the Dragon: The History Of Addiction Treatment and Recovery in America*. Illinois: Chestnut Health Systems/Lighthouse Institute.

Woititz, Janet G. 1982. *Adult Children of Alcoholics*. Deerfield Beach, FL: Health Communications.

Wolch, Jennifer R. 1996. Community-based human service delivery. *Housing Policy Debate* 7:649–671.

World Almanac. 1996. Mahah, New Jersey: Funk and Wagnalls.

Wuthnow, Robert. 1994. *Sharing the Journey*. New York: Random House.

———. 1998. *Encyclopedia of Politics and Religion*, Washington, DC: Congressional Quarterly, Inc.

Yeaton, W.H. 1994. The development and assessment of valid measures of service delivery to enhance inference in outcome-based research. Measuring attendance at self attendance of self-help group meetings: new methods in mental health research. *Journal of Consulting Clinical Psychology* 62(4):686–94.

Young, Michael. 2002. Confessional protest: the religious birth of U.S. social movements. *American Sociological Review*. 67:660–688.

Zavestoski, Stephen, Rachel Morello-Frosch, Phil Brown, Brian Mayer, Sabrina McCormick, and Rebecca Gasior Altman. 2004. Embodied health movements and challenges to the dominant epidemiological paradigm in *Research in Social Movements, Conflicts & Change* edited by Daniel Myers and Daniel Cress, 25:253–278. Oxford: JAI Press/Elsevier Science.

Index